THE ADVENTURE PARADOX

PARADOX

*How to Haul It All, Go Big & Go Home
in Your Relationships*

BY
CAT CALDWELL MYERS

Dedication

This book is dedicated to
the greats and the grands:
from my children, to my parents,
to yours, and the ones we carry in us.

A NOTE ON THE BOOK, TRIP & CHARACTERS

This book was originally written during quarantine, then refined in the spring of 2023 to serve women, mothers, and caretakers in living the life of their dreams. I hope you can read it front to back as the adventure story that it is, but also feel free to return to the teachings and chapters that most resonate with you and share them. It is an interactive tool that I use in my workshops, both virtually and in person with animals "back at the ranch" and all across the country. I invite you to let the wisdom, truth, and teachings of this journey flow through you. This is your assignment, starting now.

At the beginning of each chapter, you will see a GPS screenshot to orient you. There were a lot of moving parts, so this roadmap is designed to provide clarity. In a few cases, I have changed the actual locations to preserve anonymity, and omitted details for simplicity.

This trip would not have been possible without the unwavering help, support, and challenges brought on by my friends, family, and the people we met along the way throughout the journey. I am, and have always been, "grateful for whoever comes, because each has been sent as a guide from the beyond," as Rumi wrote in The Guest House. Anyone outside of myself is a guest in my own mind and world, and I learned to "welcome and entertain them all!" I include the whole poem in the opening to my virtual workshop which can be downloaded from my website. To preserve the anonymity of the guests I included in this text, I have changed everyone's names in the book.

If you are in this book, I just want to say THANK YOU: I

wouldn't be where I am without you! I also have no intention of hurting anyone's feelings and would like to make it right if I somehow have, so please reach out and let me know. As Allison K. Williams wrote:

> "You can't stop people from feeling their feelings and having their own memories, and you will never finish your book if you are trying to please them more than you are trying to write your story. A memoir is, by definition, one person's memory."

My intention was to write my way out of an old story and into a new one, for myself and my reader, and, God willing, anyone else who chooses to come along. In the words of Ram Das, may we all be successful in "walking each other home." I'll see you in the starry sky now – look up, my friend, then down, and take the next step in your awakening.

TABLE OF CONTENTS

Part 3:

Back at the Ranch

March 11, 2020

Suburb of Chicago

Prologue

GET OUT OF YOUR STORY

"The very reason I write is so that I might not sleepwalk through my entire life."

- Zadie Smith, author

None of us really saw quarantine coming. It's not that some people weren't following the global pandemic taking place in China and beyond, it's just that most of us hadn't quite grasped what it would mean for America, and the world at large, until we were all in the wake of the tidal wave of pandemonium leading up to it. Eventually, all of us got on board this ship to ride it out, because we realized it *was* the sea and we might otherwise drown in our fears.

True to form, I was totally absorbed in my day-to-day life with horses and young children, just following "the fear" from a distance, until it dawned on me that I better get some more hand sanitizer. It was March 10th, 2020 when I recognized how far behind the curve I was. Not only was no hand sanitizer available, disinfectant wipes, Clorox, and the like were backordered for many weeks, or even months.

I was surprised that my laissez-faire attitude had landed us in the middle of being totally unprepared for what was happening. I just hadn't quite understood how being "laid back" could hurt us until that moment. Still, my intuition reminded me to stay calm and look for the opportunities that this new way of life, and every single one of these little inconveniences, might offer.

Since the experience of birthing my children naturally, I had learned to feel my way through things, rather than thinking so hard. My need to be needed and loved at a deep level impacts me physically, mentally, emotionally, and spiritually when my child cries out. I now felt this in my very bones, beginning with pregnancy, and it made me feel closer to my own birth mother and grandmothers. The instinctual desire to be with my babies often contradicted my desire to be and do things that used to bring me joy *in the way that I used to do them.*

Prior to having children, I felt this change as a caretaker of animals and considered them my first "kids." My animals taught me to think and feel for "us," for our "family," not just for myself, as I went about my days. Even before owning animals, like most women I know and work with, I had a tendency to "take it all on" by putting the needs of others before my own.

Not taking care of yourself first will catch up to you, and on day 12 of quarantine, I finally hit a wall. I knew it was going to be rough when I woke up because I was not ready to wake up. Some of the responsibilities that I had partially delegated, like cleaning our huge house or caring for our dependents, were now 100% on me – or so I felt. These included caring for two children under age 4, four horses, a dog, a cat, a huge house with 5 acres of property, and my husband, who was now working from home, which meant we were also trying to hold his career together. The adrenaline of doing it all by myself had completely worn off – I was exhausted. This lifestyle, with young children and livestock, a total of 8 dependents, needed a village to sustain it, and to sustain me. My batteries were totally empty, just like every other young mom I knew.

One day, early on, after a few hours of helping the children play, eat, and clean up accidents here and there, I was beside myself with self-pity. I couldn't even go through the motions to get my children into a routine to get to their rooms for nap-time. It was embarrassing and scary. I felt the need to escape.

Instead of pretending everything was alright, I said aloud, "Mommy is really tired, and it would be better not to talk to me for a little while because I don't want to yell at anyone." My oldest daughter, Grace, who was four, seemed to understand perfectly and suggested that I go to my room and take a nap. I couldn't because my husband, George, was working remotely (along with everyone else in the world who could), and I needed to be responsible for our children not interrupting him. We had not found our rhythm yet in all of this.

Where was my own mom when I needed her? Sadly, many states away, and immunocompromised, so I knew I could not call on her for physical help. George's mother was within driving distance but of the age where COVID was most risky, and so I felt I could not call her either. I felt helpless, isolated, and alone, even with my children and husband there.

These feelings brought me to the edge, and yet, there was no end in sight. When would it be okay to call for help? Before or after a mental breakdown? Before or after I hurt my children or myself – emotionally, physically, or mentally? I knew better than to find out. The red flags were all around me. I was the one losing it, not my children.

It was time to resort to drastic measures. So I did. I turned on the TV. Most people might not think this is a big deal, but in my family, TV is looked at like eating chocolate or ice cream: everybody does it, and a little is okay, but too much is frowned upon. Being well-educated, I knew how dangerous too much screen time can be for the precious brains of babes. I also knew that stay-at-home mothers with children under the age of 5 are statistically the most depressed people. "Hurt people hurt people," and depressed people are hurt, and I felt like I might be experiencing symptoms of depression in myself as I had when I was postpartum. I decided to take my chances with the lesser of two evils.

When I laid down on the couch next to Grace and my younger daughter, Dani, who was two years old, I was both horrified and comforted as my four-year-old stroked my arm and said, "There, there, Mommy – you go ahead and sleep now. You'll feel better after a nap. It's ok. We'll be fine watching Pinkalicious." I drifted off to the overture: "Pink is the color that grows and grows…" Outside, the Chicago spring weather was gray and stormy.

When I woke up forty minutes later, I felt refreshed. I wiped the drool off my arm, looked up, and noticed that the sun was out now. It felt like the weather was mimicking my mood. We'd woken up to a winter wonderland, which was beautiful and confusing at the same time. "Isn't it spring?" Grace asked. "Why does it look like wintertime outside?"

Four-year-old Grace was vocalizing how the changing of the seasons can be confusing. "There's a lot of back and forth before it's really spring," I told her. The same could be true of my mood, I realized. I'd needed that commercial break for my brain, which was exhausted from the feeling that I was "doing it all."

When I considered the story of my life as it might play back on the big picture screen, it was amazing to see the many chapters. There were so many humbling and humiliating experiences that I had overcome by age 39. The first physical miracle of my life (after being born) was during my senior year in high school, when I broke my neck in a horseback riding accident. The injury resulted in my having to wear a neck brace for six months, with limited movement and abilities for another two years after that. The doctors said that I came within a fraction of being paralyzed from the neck down. This gave me a new perspective on having a fully functioning body. After that, I never took a day for granted and went after life with a zest only the dying can truly understand. Whatever opportunity I was presented with, I went after it with gusto. I knew that life was precious and there was some greater mystery at work.

It's ironic, because that life-long energy came out of an injury that required me to sit out entire seasons of sports, graduation parties, reunions, and gatherings. In some ways, quarantine was a full circle for me, personally, because I was familiar with this meditative state of "wait and see" as your body heals, so I did not struggle with staying at home in the way that many did. In fact, it was a welcome reprieve from the hustle and bustle of the suburban farm life I was living going into 2020. I had more goals, invitations, and commitments than I could possibly keep up with, even in a fully functioning body that I wasn't sure I wanted to expose to "the coronavirus." So, I sat down and reflected on where I was, where I'd been over the last five years, and where I wanted to go in five years. To overcome what felt like depression, I turned inward, in search of that mystery.

Our "shelter-in-place" family had grown a lot – physically, mentally, emotionally and spiritually – over the course of six years. In 2014, we'd left our mountain home in the West and taken out our first mortgage in Libertyville, IL. Then we'd built a horse barn with pastures on the edge of the Des Plaines River Trail, popped out two children, and added on two more horses. I found myself managing multiple helpers to cover all we had going for us, because it was more than I could do by myself. Although it was everything I'd dreamed of, I was also overwhelmed and exhausted much of the time. This did not feel like the life I'd signed up for. As I watched the last horse farms around us disappear when the horses died or neighbors sold them, I felt like the lone ranger on our small horse farm. George's corporate job and my full-time mother and caretaker duties made it even more isolating.

Why was I really here?

For me, travel is often a way of figuring this out, but I wanted to do it with all my loved ones in tow. So, in the summer of 2018, I left my suburban lifestyle behind to explore this question with a big horse road trip back out west to where my husband and I had lived a simpler life. That trip was an escape from what was, a full on adventure antidote to facing the fear of being stuck at home with young children and all the responsibilities of our small farm in a big house all summer long. Yet here I was living that supposed "nightmare" out, along with all the other young moms I knew, and I saw another opportunity to follow through on another dream.

When quarantine first started, I got an email from a friend suggesting that now was the time to get after those writing projects we had been putting on hold, and this sparked something in me. I prayed that God would give me wisdom, peace, and strength to make it through whatever this (quarantine) was, and to finally write the book I felt called to write about the trip we took. So, for an hour every day (when we thought that quarantine would only last 40 days), I sat down and wrote the stories you are about to read. It is important to understand that they were written in a time of intense uncertainty. "We see the world we feel," and I felt simultaneously triumphant at the unexpected opportunity to write and reflect on this experience, and baffled by what was really going on in "real time" with the pandemic.

WRITE, RECORD and SHARE

Use the space below to write a few sentences, or pull out your phone and record a short video. Share it with us on social media or through my website!

During Quarantine, I felt...

_____

The Standards I dropped were:

_____

The Opportunity I saw (and took) was:

_____

The Reason I am REALLY HERE today is:

_____

The Story I wish I'd started writing 5 years ago is:

_____

_____

_____

_____

_____

Congratulations – you just wrote your Quarantine Prologue! Share with us on social media, via email, or join us for The Adventure Paradox live Zoom call series as we go along.

PART I:

How to Haul It All

Before going on any adventure, we usually pack. This is a conscious act where we prepare equipment, supplies, and strategies for any possible scenarios. Having a spare tire, extra snacks, diapers, and feed for animals is essential. Of course, there is always "one more thing" to add, and even more things we don't know are coming. In the early days of this journey, I felt I had to haul it ALL (spoiler alert; you don't, by the way).

Invitation: If you want to see images of the journey and what we packed, please mosey on over to my website and check out my free workshop that includes pictures and a process to figure out what you are hauling… and what you're ready to let go of.

ZERO Miles

Spring of 2018

Libertyville, IL

SATISFACTION
BROUGHT IT BACK

"God gave YOU the dream, don't expect other people to get it – it's not their dream."

- Dougie Hall of Medicine Bucking Horses

It didn't make sense — even to me, if I'm honest – why I wanted to take such a long journey with so many challenging variables, except that I had something to prove to myself and others. Ever since moving to the midwest, I had dreamed of trailering back to the mountains with the horses for a summer. There had even been plans with old horse friends coming together for the summer of 2017, but then I ended up pregnant with my second, and plans changed. I remember thinking that if I didn't go in the summer of 2018, it was possible that I never would.

Although people tried to talk me out of it – and they had plenty of good reasons, might I add – I still just knew *I had to go*. I had to prove that there was goodness in the sake of adventure itself in any season of life. I'd struggled with not feeling good enough my whole life, and in many ways, this trip was an effort to make peace with my own crazy ideas, despite other people's opinions of them.

Not everyone was against me — I had one fan, an aging executive who got authors out in front of the media. She believed in the value of my idea and wanted me to book press conferences along the way to start getting media attention and propel me toward getting an agent. Ironically, that was almost enough to make me quit. It was in that moment that I realized how close to the edge of what we could handle this idea was: so close, in fact, that there was no way I could commit to meeting with people along the way, given the knowns and unknowns of traveling with horses, a dog, and young children across the country. So, I threw out the press release idea but kept the rest of her excitement with me, allowing her encouragement to fuel us.

I had enough to haul without this on top of it. What appealed to her most was the fact that I would have to be doing a lot of this alone, because she was facing doing a lot of things alone now that her husband was deteriorating mentally and physically. Of course, I would not be alone and knew I could not do it alone – it would take a village to make it happen, especially because my husband could not make the whole trip with his corporate job.

When I learned that he would be spending two weeks in India that summer for work, I found myself dreading being at home alone with our children and all of our animals. I was also experiencing symptoms of depression, and facing this vision made them fiercer, so I started thinking about what would make me feel better. The best antidote would be an adventure.

The thing was that we missed the west and wanted to get back there. It wasn't just the mountains, it was also our community of friends and people like us. Here in the midwest, I often felt like a fish out of water, and I thirsted for that connection to a place that I felt in the Tetons. Somehow, I believed that by taking a journey all the way out there, I would come back healed and better able to embrace the life I had. I packed this idea up, promising everyone that I was going to write a book about it. If I was paying attention

14

and creating something, perhaps the answers would come along the way (and they did). I also promised that I would come back to Hidden Ranch, and to our relatives here in the midwest.

For me, the healing often comes through the hauling of horses. We are all hauling something, like the stories that we tell ourselves, but I also like to physically haul 12,000 pounds of adventure behind me when I go. Our three-horse gooseneck steel trailer with a weekender package had been our first home, and I'd used it for another major life transition in my past. I just knew that there would be something empowering about doing it now that I had young children – not just for me, but for them – but I would need a third adult to do it, and a lot of creativity and faith.

George was super supportive, wanting me to be happy, but also wanting to do something fun together. We'd met backcountry skiing in a rescue mission on Teton pass when he was on vacation, and adventure was our middle name. Together, we laid out an itinerary with friends, horse motels, and Airbnbs bootlegged together to make it work. Unfortunately, he had that "real job" thing that meant he would be gone for 17 out of the proposed 40 days. Now we just had to think of who else might come with us for the trip of a lifetime.

When I pitched the idea to Ruthie, our 26-year-old part-time nanny who was married to a worship pastor, I was only half serious, and I half expected her to say no. After thinking it over for a weekend, she said yes! I was really surprised and thrilled but also a little bit horrified. Not having a helper was an excellent excuse that this trip wasn't meant to be, but the fact that she was "all over it" put gas in the tank when I was running on empty before, during, and after our journey.

I'd found Ruthie through the care.com website when I was 6 months pregnant with my second child. Despite being twenty-something, she was all business at our library interview, and I was immediately impressed. Of course, being a part-time professional actress, dancer, and model contributed to her wow factor, but she had depth, too. Her confidence, ideas, charisma, and passion for being a nanny were founded in the love she had for her own nanny growing up, with whom she kept in touch throughout her life. I knew we'd make an excellent team and that she would create positive experiences for my girls.

It's funny now, because I couldn't see it then, but the crux of this trip would be about relationships – not just with Ruthie, but with my husband, our children, the horses, and our wonderful dog, Chadeaux, and myself. The only way it was going to work was if I kept the faith, regardless of the circumstances, and we all stayed centered with each other and fluid in our respective roles. Our trip was like moving water, everything kept changing, but our mission was clear: "Keep everyone safe, address the needs of all creatures, hosts, and challenges posed by the weather, holiday closures, or road conditions, and stay the course to have an amazing adventure." That was our assignment.

My old truck didn't even have airbags, and my family had been begging me to upgrade. We did some research and decided to trade out my 2001 Chevy Silverado to buy a brand new 2018 RAM 2500 and immediately named her Red Beauty. The trailer got checked out, and then we started cleaning, packing, and preparing for it to "hit the road" since it had been sitting for almost three years. "Safety first" meant we needed to be sure it was ready to haul.

You see, we're all hauling something. Even when we stay home and play it safe, we end up hauling extra weight! Many Americans are suffering from "the sitting disease." I have coached women out of their seats and into a fitness routine hundreds of times, assisting them in mindset and healthy eating habits, but I still struggle with the battle of the bulge. I chuckled when my only fan, the older executive (who also had weight to lose), suggested, "You might lose 15 pounds!" At that moment, I recognized that every woman who has weight to lose, and even those who don't, have this secret fantasy that following some crazy dream might simultaneously result in a magical transformation. I'd coached women through terrible tragedies, divorces, and more, but when it came to weight gain, the greatest challenge of all was always motherhood.

I'm not sure if it's the connection to sitting and motherhood, or some other major factor, but I've given it a lot of thought. Without a doubt, a growing fetus needs to be fed, and women will generally gain weight through a healthy pregnancy, but the range of weight gained was vast, and many never returned to their pre-baby weight or lifestyles. One of my favorite studies when coaching women was recognizing how many women had gained the weight during their pregnancy, then had *never* taken it off. When I would ask how old their child was, they would smile wryly and say, "*25...*" It always caught me off guard when I realized they meant *years*, not months!

This was when I recognized it must have something to do with the habits and moods of motherhood in general – perhaps the constraints, or the constant pull on the heartstrings. Whatever it was, I was compelled not to lose myself in it and had successfully lost the 65 pounds I gained after Grace was born in about 15 months. Then, when I was finally feeling like myself again, back to a healthy weight, I got pregnant immediately and unexpectedly, and once more began to gain weight. Carrying extra weight was a bit like hauling a horse trailer – you can feel the drag on everything that you do, and you have to consider it in each turn.

It was coming off more slowly after the second baby, of course, and a lot of that was the challenge of having two children under the age of 2. I was tired and depleted all the time. The energy I used to have to do things that gave me pleasure was like a blinking Christmas tree light before it goes out, which led me to another clear fear I had around motherhood: that I would stop riding, exploring, and having adventures, just like my Grandmother said I would. I had to prove her wrong, not so much for her, but for myself and all my children, so I got off the couch and went for it. After all, "Curiosity killed the cat, but satisfaction brought it back."

WRITE, RECORD and SHARE

Use the space below to write a few sentences, or pull out your phone and record a short video. Share it with us on social media or through my website!

Do you believe you are worthy of your desires and dreams?

_____

Are you sitting through most of your day?

_____

If you are already in action, how do you manage your feelings when you have to "sit one out?"

_____

What is the next dream you will go for?

_____

Who will help you do it?

_____

Why is now the time?

_____

Congratulations – you have just identified your next dream! Now get off the couch and go take one action towards it. I'd love to hear (or see) what that is – please share your dream with me...

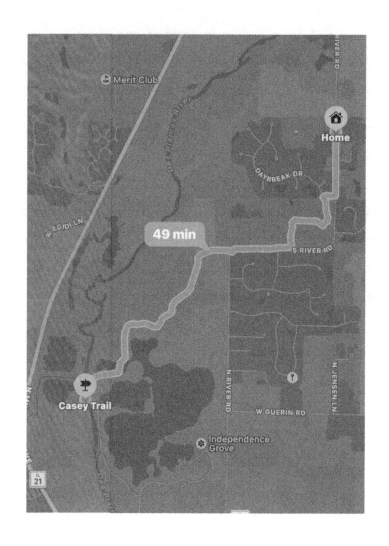

Horseback Riding

Late May, 2018

Des Plaines River Trail, IL

LOVE THE ONE
YOU'RE "ALL IN" WITH

"If I cannot fly, let me sing."

– Stephen Sondheim

Riding my horse Jet down the trail with my friend Barbie – who really did look like a dirty blonde rocker Barbie, complete with a phone carried in a stretchy case on her bicep – I was talking about the trip. She had dreams of moving out West with her own horse to New Mexico, where I grew up, but had never "trailered" a horse that far before. In between giving her pointers about how to travel long distances with one horse, I was processing my own proposed journey with three horses, two children, and my reasons for doing it.

"The thing is, I've done big horse road trips like this before, just not with kids," I said as we walked along with the clip-clop of horse hooves carrying our conversation. "I know I'll grow as a person, but I actually think my real spiritual growth would come from staying home, because being here and at home is what really challenges me. Isn't that ironic?"

She nodded, as though she understood. Then her horse stopped, shaking her mane to get the flies off, and bent down to scratch her nose on her leg. Barbie looked down at her, contemplatively, then back at me.

"It isn't easy being home with young kids, but paying someone else to raise them so you can work and go do what you want isn't easy either – that's why I chose to put my career on hold and be home with my boys so that I could be the one raising them myself. We're fortunate we both have that option." I knew she was right – this was the mother's paradox.

We began to walk again, and I felt that old familiar guilt coming on, the one where I don't feel like I deserve it, the one where *just because you can, it doesn't mean you should.* Even though I could afford to have a nanny to help me, I also knew from growing up with hired help that there is no substitute for your own mother's love. Then again, the lifestyle I enjoyed was not possible without someone to watch the children from time to time. I loved being with them, but I also loved *this* – riding – *and they could not yet do this with me.*

"Yes, I understand what you're saying; I think I'm seeking balance. I mean, I wouldn't be on a ride if I didn't have help back at the ranch watching the kids, and there is no way I could take a trip like this without help. George can't do the whole trip because of work, and I would not choose to travel as the only adult with 3 horses, a dog, and 2 kids under the age of 2. I've got to have one person on kids and one person on animals at any given time, in case there is an emergency, or I just can't do it and stay sane. It wouldn't work."

Barbie didn't say anything for a while, then she picked up her reins and chirped, "Do you wanna trot?" She actually meant *let's run 'em!* Barbie and Jordy were like that – they liked to go fast, and Jet and I were mostly game, except for his racehorse tendencies taking over his brain at times. Maybe I was more like him than not, gearing up for a race of my own… but why? As we galloped down the Des Plaines River trail, I could feel her thoughts rising up in the air like a big midwestern question mark: *"For God's sake,*

Perhaps some part of me knew the answer. It wasn't just that I needed to prove something, or that I was afraid I would never do it if I didn't do it now… it was more than that. I knew that one day, staying at home would be all I had, and that the time to spread my wings with my young children was now. Looking at all four of my 90-year-old grandparents who had been world travelers, CEOs, authors, and all-around successful contributors to humanity, I was reminded that there are many seasons to life, and parenting young children is just one of them. In the end, we would all be "going home," and "staying home."

When people ask me if I would have changed anything about the trip, I say that the one thing I would have changed was how fast we did it. We covered over 6000 miles in 40 days, and we were all exhausted at the end. Next time, I would *slowwwwww wayyyyyy* down. I'd still take at least 5-10 days to haul 2500 miles across the country with horses and young children in tow, but then I'd stay at our destination for a month or two, not a week or two, before moving on again. None of us had enough time to ever get really grounded, and this led to adrenal fatigue when we got home – a result of not having time to process each hiccup, or fear, as it came along to greet us.

Horses are great teachers of a type of empathy and compassion that transcends time. The things that scared horses 100 or 1000 years ago still scare them for the same reasons, but now there are new things, too. For example, a horse will always fear a large lion bolting towards them until they recognize that it's focused on another kill and they are safe. Today, it could be a dump truck that triggers the same fear response, followed by a deep snort through their nostrils as they realize it is not a threat to their life.

Of course, horses can stay pretty high-strung once triggered, some more than others, just like human beings.

My therapist calls this state "vigilance." I call it the "high alert mode" that comes for mothers when they have an infant, or two, and anything goes wrong, or we witness a potential for it to go wrong and latch onto that. As I planned all of the logistics for the trip, I sought the "lions, tigers, and bears" that I'd have to look out for, and how to keep my family and our animals safe through any trial.

This is where the nanny came in – she would be on children when I was on horses, so we could make sure everyone was taken care of all the time. But a nanny is not a substitute for a mother's love, and this paradox plagued me later. She was also not a substitute for my husband, either, and we would eventually find ourselves lost in the desert, with only faith to carry us through. As my full-time adventure partner, she was going to help me bring home the bacon, and she did, but not without a few "hitches in the giddyup."

WRITE, RECORD and SHARE

Use the space below to write a few sentences, or pull out your phone and record a short video. Share it with us on social media or through my website!

What is "the worst that could happen?"

_____

What is the best that could happen?

_____

What measures can you put in place to prepare for both?

_____

How do you ground yourself on the road?

_____

Do you have any routines with animals or nature?

_____

What animals and people are you responsible for (or to), even if they are not with you?

_____

How do you justify delegating caretaking duties to pursue your passions?

_____

As you look at your dream, who are the known players that will make it become a reality?

_____

Now, go share your dream with them! Your people, your animals, and your ideas about your responsibilities for them are part of your haul — congratulations on identifying them.

333 Miles

June 29th

Grand Meadow, MN

WEATHERLY ACTS OF GOD

"We don't just sing; we are the song." – Louise Penny

George was supportive of the horse road trip, but his corporate job made it impossible for him to be on the road with us for our original 35-day itinerary. In fact, he was going to be in India for almost two weeks in the middle of it, so we came up with a plan that included him flying back and forth twice. After driving across the country with us initially, he would fly home from Jackson Hole to go abroad. Then he would rejoin us in Colorado for ten days before flying back to Chicago again for work. Our nanny, Ruthie, would be with us for the entire journey and would have enough experience driving by the end to help me haul the trailer back across the country with just the two of us.

I don't remember exactly when or how Ruth told me that she had forgotten about her cousin's wedding being 3 days after our proposed departure. It was frustrating and logistically confusing to delay the whole trip because of this. After all, we had been through preparing the trailer, buying feed, and brainstorming how to keep the kids entertained for long hours on the road. I couldn't believe that we had missed this major detail, but somehow, we had.

Still, Ruthie proved resourceful and dedicated time and again, suggesting she could meet up with us at our first stop, 6 hours down the road, and do the rest of the trip. Honestly, I was almost hoping that this would be the excuse I needed to bail on the whole thing, but her enthusiasm and gesture of good faith to move forward kept me going, time and time again. We set our course to meet at a friend's farm six hours down the road from home, and four hours from the wedding, which was in a different direction.

That week, after she left, the weather started being a serious issue. We could see it about seven days out: it was going to be hot, *really hot*. Not just hot, but *humid*, too, a horrible combination for loading a bunch of horses into a metal box to go barreling down the black top road in late June.

I'd dealt with heat out West: in Nevada and California, we had seen June temperatures well over a hundred degrees while hauling. To beat the heat, we would get up a few hours before sunrise while the roads were still cool and arrive at our destination long before the hottest part of the day. Unfortunately, the added variable of humidity often made this strategy ineffective because it was sometimes hotter *before* sunrise as the dew was densest then, making it impossible to find a cool and safe window to travel in.

I was stressed by this unknown variable and began buying all kinds of gadgets to help me manage the situation, like battery operated baby monitors that would tell us the temperature in the trailer while we were driving in the truck, and portable fans to help cool the horses off. While in motion, the horses would get the "wind in their hair" effect from the trailer windows, but it might not be enough to offset the high temperatures, steel box, black top, sun, and heat they'd produce being in such tight quarters together. It was a recipe for disaster no matter how I looked at it, but we had set our course and were determined to continue, after delaying day after day as long as we could and strategizing various safety backup plans along the first leg of the journey.

With Ruthie out of the picture in those final days, we did the best we could packing up snacks and toys and all of our supplies the night before, then setting our alarms for 3 am on the last possible day we could leave, hoping to catch a "dip" in the heat. It was still way too hot, though, so we waited 2 more hours before loading up, hoping the humidity would drop with the sun. At 5 am, we called it, and one of us put the half-asleep girls into the car while the other loaded up the horses at the last possible minute. Our horses loaded happily, recognizing their three-horse slant-load gooseneck trailer as a safe haven wherever we went. Once everyone was in, we immediately hit the road.

Between snoozing in the passenger's seat with my head tossed back to the heavens and mouth open wide, as though I hoped to catch a prayer or an angel between my lips, I checked the temperature monitor in the trailer. When it reached 99, the baby monitor broke... perhaps because no baby could or should survive being subjected to a 100-degree room. Concerned that we'd only been driving about 2 hours, with an hour of direct sunlight on them, we pulled over to see how the horses were doing at a gas station.

They were hot – *wayyyyyy* too hot. I could tell by reaching through the drop-down windows to feel their chests between their front legs, which is like a human's armpit. We unloaded them on the blacktop as quickly as we could. Then, as if on cue, the wind immediately picked up, in answer to our prayers. I watched Jet's mane and tail lift while he looked wearily at the rainbow-colored flags whipping against the fireworks tent. It was a few days before the 4th of July, and you could feel the energy of the holiday, even though no one was there to sell anything at 7 am. Two-year-old Grace was awake and helped pour out water buckets for the horses in her toddler onesie. It was great to see her beginning to participate in addressing the needs and concerns of our animals on the road, as well as her own. Baby Dani continued to sleep through it all in the truck with the air conditioner going.

After Jet took a long drink of water, grazed a bit, and stopped steaming, we knew we were in the clear. The mares seemed to be okay, but Jet was going to be the one to watch with the heat, because of his predisposition to colic. We loaded up again and continued west, northwest. I considered how unnatural traveling at high speed in a metal box is, especially for an animal that is so grounded by its hooves on the ground. Even for humans, it was all so fast, perhaps too fast.

I began worrying whether or not we would make it to our destination and started calling some boarding stables I had contacted that would be a few hours closer – perhaps 5-6 hours was too ambitious with this heat. If we could wait it out for 6-8 hours and let the horses into some pens until the heat subsided, I'd feel better. The children were fine in the AC; it was the safety of our horses in this heat that was my chief concern.

None of the horse motels I called were able to offer us an outdoor turnout. They had indoor stalls with fancy fans and fancy price tags, which a good option if they were seriously overheating. We pulled over again, having decided to check every half hour to make sure we were on the right trajectory. The well-being of our animals in the steel trailer became my obsession from the air-conditioned truck.

The horses were fine now, and I realized *it was just me being vigilant.* I lashed out at my husband about something stupid, and he called me on it. We had both been awake well into the night for many days leading up to departure, and we were not at our best. I apologized, and he let it go.

By the time we were pulling out the detailed directions to find our friend's farmland, the weather had leveled out, the horses had had several healthy checks, and we had totally regained our composure and sense of humor. Two-year-old Grace was very excited about the Goldfish we had produced to eat, baby Dani was asleep, and things seemed to be going according to plan. We touched base with Ruthie, who let us know that she was on track to arrive that evening from her family wedding, and all was well… until it began to rain… a lot. This wasn't *just* rain, this was enough to float Noah's Ark. Farmers say, "If you think a drought is bad, wait until you *live through a flood,*" and we were about to understand why.

WRITE, RECORD and SHARE

Use the space below to write a few sentences, or pull out your phone and record a short video. Share it with us on social media or through my website!

Do you believe that everything is happening for you?

_____

How do you prepare for the weather?

_____

Do you work with "Acts of God" or resist them?

_____

What prayer, phrase, or thought helps you "roll with it?"

_____

How do you let go when a worry is no longer relevant?

_____

How do you take care of your animals' and childrens' needs in the weather?

_____

At this point in your story, I want you to reflect on someone you have weathered a storm with (physically, mentally, emotionally, or spiritually). Reach out and thank them. Share the wisdom you gleaned from the experience together.

Major Storm

June 29th

Private Farm in MN

THE FIREWORKS SHOW

"There are always going to be bad things.

But you can write it down and make a song out of it."

– Billie Eilish

When you hang out with horses, you become more aware of nature's cues, since they are acutely aware of them. Some people believe that a horse knows what is going to happen about 4 days before it happens. I've always witnessed at least a 24–48-hour weather forecast in their dispositions, with the last 1–12-hour window creating the biggest impact. For example, if it's been sunny, and a weird spring snowstorm is scheduled for two days out, it will be in that half-day window before the storm starts that I'll notice my horse is a little bit on edge – skittish, or more jumpy and excitable than usual, but perhaps their disposition changes even sooner than that. Without a doubt, wind has always been a factor that excites horses, though I believe any major temperature swing or environmental change will do it, and a good handler learns to co-regulate with their horse and the weather.

It's not just their emotional state either, they respond mentally and physically as well. I could tell that our horses were stressed on the way up by their sweat and diarrhea, which should have been coming out in the shape of the soft spongy tennis balls we call manure. When we first moved from our beautiful mountain pasture home in Idaho to an old barn with two locked-up warmbloods in the suburbs of Chicago, Jet responded by losing weight, half of his mane, and becoming visibly depressed. Horses are incredibly sensitive to their environments, just like humans. The difference is, humans are the last ones to know that the weather is affecting them – dependent on the weatherman, and sometimes figuring it out days after the fact – while horses know days before it happens, perhaps. I've learned to work with them and nature to know and anticipate what is needed within hours, if not days. We also have this innate nature in us, something that I lost sight of in the midst of everything.

So there we were, smelling the rain blowing in on the breeze, which had followed the miserable heat wave we endured to get here. Our horses were happy, with food and water and space to run after such a grueling first day. Soon, their dry turn out would be a muddy pasture. The truck and trailer were parked along with a lot of other trucks and trailers on the farmland that stretched for miles all around with huge silos. Everything felt right with the world, although the storm was definitely coming, and we could feel the imminent charge in the air, with an oppressive dark rain cloud looming overhead!

We were tired from the trip there, and all the added stress that had come with the heat, while our children were ready to play. Our hosts agreed to watch them so we could get ourselves sorted out before the storm hit. As I walked to the trailer, I realized I was too late. The horses were galloping back and forth, bucking and whinnying, and I could see the white squall blowing toward us.

As it began raining cats and dogs, I ran for cover in the cab of the truck – even the trailer couldn't provide solid shelter from this wind and rain. As I sat there, looking out at the now blurry landscape – a moving Monet, if you will – I reflected on the first 24 hours of our trip. They had been hard, at best, and horrible at worst. Why was I doing this?

Our friends, the Bauers, had the same reaction, as we shared all of our trials and tribulations. "You know, it isn't too late to change your mind," they said. "You could just turn around and go straight home and we wouldn't love you any less."

"Yes, of course, I know that," I said. "But I think you're missing the point: the hard part is over! We are finally on the road now, and the rest will be easy, especially once we have another adult on board to share the load of child care and animal care."

The Bauers had been instrumental in helping us set a date for departure. Originally, we had planned to spend a few more days with them, but the weather had put a kibosh in our plans, as we kept delaying and waiting for a break in the heat that was only now coming upon arrival. We'd met in birth class when we were both pregnant with our firsts. The instructor had asked how we managed stress, and when Lisa Bauer said, "I just go out and pet my pony," I knew we would be fast friends. She had grown up on this farm, with all her cousins riding horses, and it was fun to put the pieces of where she came from together. Her mom was also a horse woman who I was just getting to know and who had generously given our herd pasture.

As her parents took us in like family, we felt all the comforts of home, which was especially welcome with the harsh weather outside. Everyone was gathered for an annual 4th of July neighborhood fireworks party. It had been going on for years, and I had heard so much about it that actually being there felt surreal. Many of them had gotten their Pyrotechnic Expert certifications so that what they were doing was legal, and it had also allowed them to go bigger and better every year, always building on what they had learned from the last "show."

Sadly, one of their founding members, a neighbor, had passed away unexpectedly, and this year was about honoring him. My friend, Lisa, had undergone a scare with breast cancer, and I knew every adventure we shared was a gift. I was touched by the fact that life is so precious and that it keeps going for the rest of us long after our loved ones are gone, though it will never be the same without them. I was also aware of the beauty inherent in how people come together to celebrate those we have lost and honor them in unique ways.

This combined with the downpour outside made the mood of the group both somber and excitable. We were a mirror of the horses who went from galloping and bucking up and down their paddock to shivering together to build heat in the shelter. It all seemed to be going according to plan — some greater plan that none of us humans could quite understand, though it was slowly dawning on us that the fireworks show might not happen that night with the rain. Still, we played out various scenarios in preparation as the rain continued.

During the long waiting game that ensued, Ruthie arrived with her mother and grandmother, at the end of their own 5- or 6-hour drive from her cousin's wedding. Having someone there to attend to our children so we could be present to the situation and our friends felt amazing. It allowed us the space we needed to consider what made sense given the circumstances with the horses and the fireworks. The truth is, horses are a lot like fireworks — things go beautifully if you know what you are doing, but that takes a lot of steps and training, and even then, sometimes things "go off" when they're "not supposed to," and people can get hurt. I assured her that they had seen plenty of fireworks, but she pointed out that this was a much grander and louder scale that would be going off practically above their turn out, and that she would feel better if they were a few miles down the road, locked up in a trailer to be sure they were safe. I agreed, and we made a plan.

Unfortunately, our own trailer was full of 50-pound bags of feed that had been in the bed of the truck originally, but were now opened up to dry in the part of the trailer where the horses would go. She offered to use her brand new aluminum stock trailer instead, and I agreed. We loaded them up, and I followed her in someone's Jeep that would drive us back once the horses were parked down the road. Unlike our old, heavy steel trailer, I could hear the rattling of the aluminum trailer rolling over the dirt road, even with all the windows closed in the Jeep. I didn't like it, and I was concerned my horses didn't either.

When we finally arrived at our destination, I got out and put my hand through the horizontal prison bars of the stock trailer to touch them. They were all shaking like leaves, and I used my breathing and my voice and the gentle connection of my hand to calm them down while we waited for the decision about the fireworks. This wasn't good. They'd been through enough torture already, and we weren't even a full day into this unGodly trip. What if everything I was putting them through resulted in side effects of stress that could kill them? This was one of my worst fears, and I did not even want to think about it. Breathing with my hand on them, I kept the faith and thought about other things, assuring them all was right with the world.

It was getting late, and it still wasn't clear whether or not this show was happening. I was almost hoping that it wouldn't at this point. It was the same part of me that did not want this whole road trip to happen, but here we were, on the road, trusting that it was supposed to, and doing our best every step of the way.

Finally, we got the radio call: the immediate family of the deceased had decided to reschedule the show, as it was too wet in the field to place the fireworks. I texted Ruth that she should go to her hotel to sleep, and we slowly drove my horses back to their safe pasture for the night, without any more fireworks to think about. After a very long day, it was time for bed, and we had the blessing of having our first night ever sleeping as a family in our friend's RV, which was a dream come true for us, first because we were tired from the day and second because this was the type of thing we had wanted to do for a long time; get out with our family and sleep "on the road."

WRITE, RECORD and SHARE

Use the space below to write a few sentences, or pull out your phone and record a short video. Share it with us on social media or through my website!

When and why do you decide to call it off, or do you let others decide this for you?

_____

Who is in charge of your destiny, and that of your animals or children?

_____

Are you in tune with the changing weather?

_____

How do you go with the flow and adapt?

_____

When the show must go on, why do you do it?

_____

Now we are really getting into the thoughts and beliefs that guide you as things happen in your story. Keep going to change them and understand which ones drive you to heal.

787 Miles

June 30th

Pukwana, SD

THE MAGIC OF THE LAND

"Think about the word destroy. Do you know what it is? De-story. Destroy. Destory. You see. And restore. That's re-story. Do you know that only two things have been proven to help survivors of the Holocaust? Massage is one. Telling their story is another. Being touched and touching. Telling your story is touching. It sets you free."

- Francesca Lia Block, author

In the morning, Lisa was surprised that we hadn't decided to turn back that morning, given how hard things had been already. Her family stood at the end of their driveway in the middle of the country, framed by silhouetted silos, waving and talking about how crazy it was for us to continue. As they grew smaller in our rear-view, I reflected on another conversation we'd had.

A month before, when Dani had been baptized on the shore of Lake Michigan at "the church on the beach," Lisa met many of our local relatives, as well as my parents who were visiting. I learned that my mom had told her, "We'd all thank you if you could talk her out of it for us." Perhaps my friend felt she had failed on some level. Ironically, one's failure is often another's success.

Despite all odds, we persevered. That first night went off without a hitch. It was like clockwork. The weather and mood improved as we drove West through South Dakota. After one wrong turn where George had to practice turning the trailer around on a tight country road, narrowly avoiding a big ditch, we found our first official "horse motel." Through a website by the same name, we had access to a whole world of horse people, families, ranches, and private farms prepared to host equine travelers for a fee. This online source was my ticket to find hay, pasture, shavings, vets – my tribe, if you will – and I cherry picked a route paved with new horse friends and backup folks along the way.

The old man who showed up to collect payment at our first site was clearly from the grain around here. Although he drove up in a hardy canopied 4-wheeler, it was evident that he was used to another kind of ride. His weathered hands were red and leathery, gripping the steering wheel as he explained that he'd been a bull and bronc rider, among other popular rodeo events. Under his ball cap and sunglasses, both of which must have been from the 80's, you could only tell his age by his hide.

"Mostly it's just my old rodeo friends who come along and use this arena now," he said. "Every so often, we get someone like you passing through who finds us on horsemotel.com. My daughter-in-law set that up. I don't really know how to do all that stuff, but I'm glad you found us — not many people do."

As I paid him cash for boarding our horses in his arena for one night, we got to talking about the landscape. It had felt like we were really on the brink of greatness, as we had left the midwestern farmlands behind us and touched the long, slow climb toward the Rockies the day before, an area locals fondly refer to as "the black hills." You still couldn't see the "purple mountains majesty," only the hint of what lay beyond them in their grooved lava rocks, budding cliff bands, and emerging dryness that comes with altitude as gravity pulls the water down to the flatlands. We weren't technically there yet, but you could feel the flavor of the west calling us, and this character sitting before me was a perfect specimen of what I was looking for. He was just so real.

My mind drifted back to him telling me about various battles that were fought between his pioneering family over the past four generations and the Native Americans who were here first. It was clear that he felt a kinship for his Native American brothers, a camaraderie even, leaving behind any animosity his forefathers might have felt.

"They're my friends, the Dakotas. Good people. And they sure do know a thing or two about horses," he said. "When we had a problem with one, we'd take it to the elders, and they'd whisper to them in another language until they weren't a problem anymore. It's something the white man can't really learn – they are so deep with the earth and the animals, having been a part of this land for thousands of years. My four generations on this land are nothing compared to our neighbors, though I do have more respect, honoring the old ways of living here, than some of the new guys," he said, shrugging.

I loved this man and his story, his simple way of being and seeing the world. After he left, I realized he'd never even stood up or got out of the "side by side" during our entire exchange, and I wondered, in hindsight, if he even could help. I wondered if he was even older and wiser than he appeared, a disguised elder himself.

He was clear about what mattered – his children and grandchildren taking on the family land, not just as a business, but as an identity, and a shared stewardship with those who had come before them. While we never saw or met any of his relatives, I had spoken to his daughter-in-law on the phone to find the place and heard her deep in the midst of her own domestic tale with children crying and asking for things in the background. I thanked my lucky stars for the opportunity to be a nomadic family and to share these experiences of being on the road together – not because my children would remember it, but because it would shape me as a young parent forever.

Our decision four years earlier in 2014 to move back to the Chicago area from our mountain home in Teton Valley hadn't come lightly, but when it was time to go, it all just seemed to come together. Despite having family in the midwest, I'd only ever lived there for a few years of my adult life, having spent the rest of it west of the Mississippi, or abroad. I chose homes in the mountains with people who deeply valued the culture of the great outdoors and generally disdained domestic roles or metropolitan areas. But my husband's immediate family all lived within ten miles of each other, and between the two of us, we had about 30 relatives in the Chicago area. As we looked towards growing a family, we agreed that being near lots of family, diversity, and career opportunities was more important than being in the mountains, but this was a huge sacrifice.

Moving had not changed the fact that I identify as a mountain person, and I yearned to share this passion with my children, knowing that in the mountains, I am my best self. Since moving to the midwest, I had not felt like myself. Then again, I was either pregnant or nursing the whole time we had lived there, and "my self" was no longer my own. Everything about what I was and what I felt had to do with an "us." It had been my mission to become a hybrid mountain midwestern version of myself, which I did. But as soon as she learned to form the words, Grace began asking, "Mommy, why are you not happy?"

My two year old could clearly see that it was this place, these people, and, ultimately, me. I was the one who needed to change, to mold into a different version of my best "suburban horse mom" self in the midwest if this was going to work, and it would be an inside job. The whole point was to go there and back. But I could feel the "set up" already within my own soul, as I clearly hung my hat on one being better than the other, and making me "happier," in simpler terms. In the mountains, I was starting to feel at home in myself again: these were my people, this was my place. Now it was time to find my voice again and make sense of all that was and would be. In shamanic culture, they ask 4 questions to discover the depth of an illness:

- When did you last dance?

- When did you last sing?

- When did you last sit in silence?

- When did you last allow yourself to be taken in by magical stories?

I could feel my heart beginning to sing, and the peace that comes from being ready to lay down your sword and just stay a while. The adrenaline of getting out of dodge was wearing off, and the joy of the journey and the mountains and friends to come was growing stronger. But the perspective coming for me might not hold the simple healing recipe I yearned for. Like the Native American and pioneering tensions that painted the history of this landscape, it was going to be more complicated than that.

WRITE, RECORD and SHARE

Use the space below to write a few sentences, or pull out your phone and record a short video. Share it with us on social media or through my website!

What landscape does your highest self belong in?

_____

Is your extended family more alike or different than you?

_____

Do you have a chosen family?

_____

Where, and with whom, do you spend most of your time?

_____

Do you feel that you are in the place and with the people where you most belong?

_____

If not, what is keeping you from moving or changing company?

_____

Journal about the 4 questions of the Shaman now:

Dance:_____

Sing:_____

Silence: _____

Stories: _____

This is where the magic begins – you are over halfway through the first part of your story. Now you can finally begin to see what might be dragging you down and begin to let go in order to see a new story ahead. Write on...

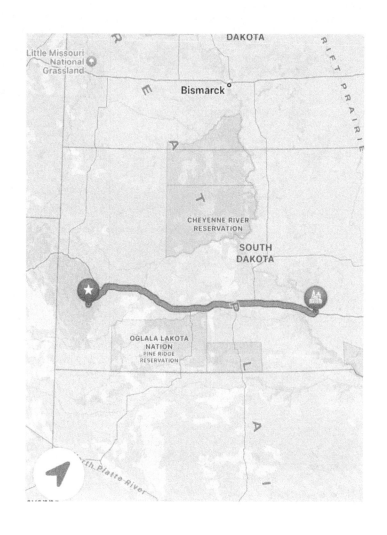

1369 Miles

July 1st

Keystone, SD

OUR DREAM TRAILER

"You have a grand gift for silence, Watson. It makes you quite invaluable as a companion."

- Arthur Conan Doyle (Sherlock Holmes)

George was driving. It was our third day on the road, heading West, and we'd been driving for a few hours already. Today was the day things were supposed to get fun – we had a rest day planned at a horse camping hotel near Mount Rushmore that looked pretty cool. I found this site through a blog connected to US Rider, which is basically "Triple A (AAA) for horse people." Not only will they bail you and your horses out of any accident or roadside closure, they'll find safe pastures and hotels and ways to fix all parts of your truck and trailer. Little did we know, our membership would be worth its weight in gold on this journey.

We pulled into a gas station, a busy one off I-90, that had huge semis and other trucks and trailers. There was a gorgeous horse camping trailer pulling out as we pulled in, and I took a photo of it, saying, "You see that trailer, Ruthie – that is the kind of trailer we want!" It was clear that with the addition of a third horse and two children and a nanny, we had quickly outgrown our three-horse trailer with a gooseneck honeymoon camper suite. It had been perfect for the two of us and our two horses to take adventures in "back in the day." We used to use the third "bay" to store hay, but now we were at capacity with three horses, and storage of hay was only the tip of the iceberg of our problems. It was as though we were literally "too big for our britches."

This trailer had a hay rack up on top of the trailer with a ladder and a cover – after years of rigging bales up in the third bay in the back, this looked like a dream come true. Some of them even had electric elevators to get the hay up and down, which only seemed silly until you dealt with trying to get 50-60 pound hay bales up and down a vertical ladder attached to the side of a trailer. You could also tell that the living quarters included *a full kitchen, full storage units, and a bathroom,* while ours just had a sink, a bed, a cupboard closet, and a cowboy shower (which is akin to the handheld sprayer you find at your sink) in the back of the trailer where the horses go. I'd never actually used it. I had, of course, used the sink as a toilet when in a bind, and washed it out and sanitized it with wipes. It was crude, but it had also been my favorite way of being "out there." Now that we had young children and a nanny traveling with us, I could see that my old newlywed shenanigans no longer made sense. I dreamed of having an actual toilet with an actual sink and shower where we could clean up and keep going, wherever we were.

Gone were the days of backcountry camping, and "in" were the days of poop and diapers and lessons on proper hand washing and hygiene – lessons that had to be continually monitored and modeled. It would be much easier to do this in a proper environment, as Montessori had observed. I knew that we couldn't count on the trailer to serve our whole group. We would take turns sleeping in it with two sets of bedding, but at least one hotel room, camp facility, or house with a working restroom, another bed, and shower would be necessary at all times... Unless we had a dream trailer like that.

I was lost in thought when I realized George had pulled up to the pump on the wrong side. We'd been waiting at this trucker's stop for a bay to open up for about 15 minutes, and it's not easy to turn a rig around under such busy conditions. I snapped out of my daydream and snapped at my partner. He returned the favor as he pulled around the gas station and down a hill with no apparent plan other than to exit the vehicle and situation.

Realizing we were not in a good place as a couple, Ruthie suggested that she would take the girls into the gas station and figure out lunch and bathrooms while we decided what to do next. I gave her my credit card and also got out of the trailer to blow off steam. Looking around to see how on earth we would back the rig up this hill, I was overcome by the faint whisper of a creek running down below, under a tree with shade and green grass. It was perfect.

"Put it in park," I said, "we can unload the horses here and have a picnic with them outside of the trailer for a little while. After lunch, we can back it up this hill empty and turn it around to load. Hopefully the crowd will clear to get gas later."

The hill was pretty steep, which was part of what we were fighting about, but the whole thing was clearly a sign that we were both burned out and exhibiting all the classic symptoms of "halt:" hungry, angry, lonely, and tired. If I hadn't gotten out of the truck to scout the area, I wouldn't have seen the beautiful solution that his "mistake" provided us. But first we had to finish our fight. While Ruthie was inside with the girls, we got the horses out and watered them and texted back and forth with her about what kind of sandwiches we wanted. One of us would need to go in to help her carry stuff out with the two young girls, but we had time to chat for a minute first.

"Maybe this is too much," I said at last. I'd been holding my breath, but I had to let it out and shine a light on the fact that we were at our edge – the edge of what our relationship could honestly handle. Ruthie, the children, and the animals seemed to be okay, but *we weren't* – we were struggling, and we weren't even 4 days into our 40-day odyssey. "Maybe we should just go back. It's possible that we have bitten off more than we can chew."

"But we've hardly even gotten anywhere," George said after a long silence.

I could tell he was committed to see it through and make it to our old stomping grounds. After all, this was his *vacation*, and he had a flight out of Jackson Hole waiting for him in 5 days. From there, he would fly back to Chicago for 48 hours, then to India for work for 10 days. Eventually, he'd return to meet us in Colorado after about 2 weeks apart. It had seemed like a dreamy idea to be out West with our old friends, engaging in an all-out adventure with our horses and children while he was away… back on the road again… until now.

Now it was clear that things just weren't lining up. This whole thing was not worth sacrificing the sanctity of our marriage. It didn't *feel like a vacation*, it felt like work – the kind of work that takes you to the breaking point. We had a tendency to "max out of the meter" on this kind of extreme travel when it was just us, and it usually took us to each other's throats.

"Let's eat lunch and talk about it after we've eaten," he proposed.

In agreement once more, I stood with the horses grazing while he went inside to help Ruthie with the children and the food. The horses didn't seem bothered by our mood. They were happy to be out of the trailer, posing for the occasional photo from interested passers-by, just being themselves in this small patch of nature behind a gas station. I offered them some water and then secured them to trees in shade so we could eat without having to worry about them running off. It was good to be out on the road with them. The new one, Tiki, was taking it all in, following the lead of Jet and Solita that this was just a normal and natural way of life. Chadeaux (our family dog) laid down on a blanket, anticipating "ground morsels" from the children, and all seemed right with the world.

Once the children joined us, things got even better. I nursed Dani and recognized that some of my "intensity" might have derived out of being "hormonal" as much as the other 4 things in halt. My lactation consultant had taught me that many women have a grumpy feeling, sort of like PMS, as their milk comes in, when they need to nurse. It had been about 4 hours since we'd left the hotel that morning, so I was grateful to serve my child and let off a little tension myself in this natural symbiotic relationship. Doing so always reminded me how closely connected a mother is with her children and contributed to feeling better and better about the whole situation.

As we sat around in camp chairs by the creek at the bottom of the hill, we apologized to Ruthie for our fight, but she was unperturbed. It was pretty bad – *had she seen worse?* Then we explained that we had been discussing whether or not this was a good idea to continue, then asked for her opinion. She felt like we could do it, and we agreed, saying a prayer together before continuing west.

Ultimately, if God was *with us*, anything was possible. The thing was, I couldn't tell *where* He was. Was this all our own *ego?* Sometimes clarity comes by doing, so we ventured on to find out.

Half an hour later, we left the freeway to follow a highway that turned into miles and miles of circular horse country roads painted in bright red dirt. When we pulled into our campsite in the black hills, we saw the "pot of gold" at the end of the rainbow. There, right behind our campsite, *was the dream trailer that we had seen* 3 hours before at the gas station where we almost turned back. Surely, it was a sign.

WRITE, RECORD and SHARE

Use the space below to write a few sentences, or pull out your phone and record a short video. Share it with us on social media or through my website!

What prayers or practices do you have in place when the going gets tough between people?

_____

When you end up in a bad spot, how do you recover?

_____

Do you take personal responsibility or place blame more?

_____

What is my version of the dream horse trailer that I believe would make my life even better?

_____

Is my money and my work using me, or am I using it to fulfill the dreams and desires that are my destiny?

_____

When I have_____, then I can have _____

Your ultimate escape or adventure may be five years out from now, but this deep work today will help you get there. Dig in! I'd love to hear or see what you have come up with — please join me on social media.

Horse Camping Site

July 2nd

Near Mount Rushmore

WORKING REMOTELY

"You're never going to kill storytelling, because it's built in the human plan. We come with it."

- Margaret Atwood, author of *The Handmaid's Tale*

Our horses were relieved to get out of the trailer and happily swished their tails in their shaded pens. We wanted to get them out on the trail to see Mount Rushmore. I'd seen it before when I moved out West from Chicago about a decade earlier and had been both impressed and perplexed by its very existence.

In fact, I became fascinated by the story of how it came into being and how it was never really finished. Why did it exist at all? How did Native Americans and patriots feel about it? How did I feel about it? Eventually, I put the analysis aside and simply allowed myself to appreciate it as a challenging work of art. I wanted to share it with our children as a snapshot of exactly what America is, up close and personal, in the living history of all her shame and glory. Sometimes what we are building is always in a state of being built. Just like travel, you never really reach your destination, just a resting place before moving on.

George and I rounded a hilltop with Jet and Solita after a long climb and finally saw it, barely. The fact that you could see it was clearly a selling point, not an impressive view. I held my fingers up: it was about the size of my pinky nail – a profile of the founding fathers in the distance.

My husband was getting bombarded with calls from work and

said he needed to respond to an email. We pulled over and let the horses graze at a high point where he had reception. So this is it, I thought. Here we come all this way, finally get out on a ride, only to have George spend 45 minutes working while we are here. I knew that this trip wouldn't be about riding. After all, our horses would be exhausted mentally, physically, and emotionally by the travel itself. Every hour of hauling is equivalent to an hour of walking down a trail for them, so even though we capped it at 4-6 hours of active hauling, these were long rides across the country, and we wanted to keep this "ride" under 3 hours. This was good for them – they were happy grazing. Mount Rushmore was too far away to see in the saddle, anyway. They'd said it was a 5-hour ride one way to get a better look, I later learned.

Ultimately, everyone was getting their needs met – even me. Clearly, I needed to just chill out and let it be. George worked, Ruthie babysat the kids. Chadeaux and our old trail horses took in the scenery and the grassland while our newest horse, Tiki, worked through being left alone, back at the ranch, which was also good for her: she needed to work through her herd-bound feelings through social distancing practices, and Ruthie and the girls were keeping an eye on her in her pen along with the rest of the horse campers, and our new dream neighbors.

We were horse camping, finally, with our family. This was the dream, right? So why was I not happy? Why did I think that this would be "it?" I was having trouble getting in touch with what I was actually feeling. Then I recognized it: I was truly exhausted. We had been running on stress hormones for months now. "Fail to plan for exhaustion and you plan to fail when it hits you," was all I could think.

After recharging our batteries with camp fuel, I just felt like we weren't there yet. I wanted to get closer to the mountains that I loved – to touch them and breathe them into my soul. The camping was as hard as I thought it would be, and I knew the only way was through. If we pushed through and skipped the scheduled rest day here, we'd be able to be in a home with our friends in Bozeman who also had kids on the 4th of July. We had to keep going. Not surprisingly, all 3 adults agreed, fueled by adrenaline, perhaps.

WRITE, RECORD and SHARE

Use the space below to write a few sentences, or pull out your phone and record a short video. Share it with us on social media or through my website!

What drives you to work through exhaustion?

_____

When I'm truly happy, I feel

_____

What would an aligned career & dream look like?

_____+_____

Are you content with just chilling or always striving to get somewhere?

_____

Do you have a balance in your dream?

_____

So many people began working remotely in the pandemic and discovered the challenges of having your work with you wherever you go. While working for yourself is the dream for many, it comes with its own challenges, which you just tapped into in this chapter — congratulations! We haul our career, and our ideas about it, wherever we go — now let's keep going.

Supposed Rest Day

July 3rd & 4th

Keystone, SD

ADRENAL FATIGUE

"We are, as a species, addicted to story. Even when the body goes to sleep, the mind stays up all night, telling itself stories."

- Jonathan Gottschall, The Storytelling Animal

On what was supposed to be our first rest day in the wilderness, I found myself wondering how my Grandma JoJo was doing. She had repeatedly called me on the horse road trip about "the white rug." We all knew that she was losing her mind, but sometimes I wondered if the reason wasn't Alzheimers but rather her obsession with who would get what as they moved out of their home of 47 years. For example, we'd had the same conversation about the white rug at least 6 times, and the fact that I couldn't do anything about it now, because, "Remember, I'm way out West with this family horse road trip?"

"Oh, that's right," she'd say. "You know, I thought about going with you..." and we'd both chuckle. I loved her sense of humor about the wild ride I was on, and her lack of judgment or concern about what we were doing. All she cared about was how I was going to take good care of her famous 10 by 20 foot white rug that had served her all those years as a corporate housewife. "You know it's really hard to keep clean," she'd say. "I always had to keep the children out of there – that will be hard for you, but sadly, no one else wants it, so I guess you'll have to do the same."

It was my turn to chuckle, because I knew about "the nice room" from my uncle Tom, who swore he would never have a room in his house that "the residents weren't allowed to use unless guests were present." The way he saw it, the living room where the white rug resided was really an extra large "guest room," and he wasn't a child when they moved in there, he was a teenager, and the resentments had clearly followed him into adulthood. Honestly, I didn't think I'd be able to keep a white rug very clean – after all, we live on a farm – but I was honored to try and have a keepsake from my grandmother that was so special to her and spoke volumes of a time gone by.

Time was passing on our trip, too. Slowly. Perhaps too slowly as we got up early and made the decision to do a double shift in order to get to our friends by nightfall for a 4th of July BBQ. We were on the fifth full day of our journey. It had taken longer than we'd expected to get our campsite packed up, and it was looking tight to get there by dinner; fireworks might be more realistic since it was more likely we'd get there by nightfall.

At dinner time, we pulled over to get gas, water the horses in the trailer, and order a pizza at the Dominos across the way. Everything was closed because it was the 4th of July, so pickings were slim. As I walked back to the truck to feed Chadeaux and walk her around a bit, I noticed that one of our trailer tires was cocked at a funny angle – a really funny angle. It was off. I'm not a mechanic, but I could tell it didn't look right, and I was alarmed about the big mountain pass looming ahead of us.

Of course, we were far from home, and it was a holiday. I knew I couldn't call any of those guys — we needed to find help where we were: "Bloom where you're planted," as they say. I said a silent prayer and looked around the parking lot while our pizzas cooked. Sure enough, a man in a huge rig had just pulled up. I couldn't tell what kind of a truck it was, but it had a crane attached, and I figured the driver might know more about my tire and the accompanying axles than I did, so I approached him casually.

He was writing something in a book of some sort with his driver's door held open by his boot, about 6 feet above me. "Excuse me," I said, in my coolest *damsel in distress who can still hold it together and ask for help* voice. "You look like you know a thing or two about rigs. There's something weird going on with the tire on my horse trailer – would you mind taking a look?" He peered down at me over his glasses, like Santa Claus trying to decide whether I'd been naughty or nice.

"Where is it?" he asked gruffly, from a mouth buried beneath a shaggy brown beard.

"Right over there," I said, gesturing to our trailer parked about 40 feet away from him in the same parking lot.

"Oh sure," he said. "Let me just finish my work log, and I'll be right over."

Satisfied, I went back to the point of concentration and petted the horses while we waited. The next thing I knew, he was yanking on my tire and a whole posse of other gentlemen in orange construction vests began showing up with matching trucks. All of them were congregated around our tire seamlessly, carrying the right tools without even being told what was needed.

"Who are you guys?" I asked, incredulous.

"We're train mechanics, ma'am," one of them answered happily, as more men gathered around us to investigate. "This is definitely off," he said. "Your tires look like the tread isn't wearing evenly on them, too – you'll probably need to replace them before your trip is over."

"But I just replaced them before the trip!" I said aloud, realizing that might not be true... maybe it was before we moved 4 years ago. Still, I knew I'd had the tread checked out, but it dawned on me that that was over 2,000 hot miles ago. 2,000 miles that we had hauled with over 6,000 pounds of horses and supplies in tow on top of the 8,500-pound trailer itself. I made a "note to self" about the tires.

Meanwhile, the mechanic explained to me that my axles were running hot. They showed me how to loosen the hubcap and spit on the axle. If the spit boiled, or sizzled at all, it was too hot. It should be warm, but not hot enough to "cook an egg."

"If it's boiling after about 70 miles, then you should reconsider driving that pass tonight. You may want to come up with a plan B. Also, don't go over about 65 miles per hour – better to play it safe, just in case." They tightened a few bolts and refused to let us buy them dinner. "Let the man pay for that," they guffawed, "after all, he's the one making us work a holiday!"

I thanked them for their help and the assurance that we'd be safe as long as we kept checking it. "You can always slow down to about 50 and try to keep going." Their wisdom spoke volumes, but I was still annoyed that we were only 2 hours from our destination, yet traveling 30 below the speed limit would make it another 3 hours at least. The story of the axle running hot was not over, but we didn't know that yet...

As we slowly made our way back to the freeway, the most beautiful sunset spread out before us. There were fireworks going off in every direction that we could see — like sparkling green palm trees, shooting stars, with the usual red, white, and blue streamers. "In God We Trust," I thought as we drove to the mountains and into the darkness, but right now, I wasn't sure I trusted Him — or was it me? Was I like Grandma trying to micro-manage all the details without trusting that it would all work out as God planned? Had I really brought God with me, or was I hauling Him in name only, like American money?

WRITE, RECORD and SHARE

Use the space below to write a few sentences, or pull out your phone and record a short video. Share it with us on social media or through my website!

Am I chasing a holiday or deadline by which to make something happen?

_____

How is this working for me?

_____

Am I motivated by deadlines or are they too stringent?

_____

How does your nationality influence your thoughts on money?

_____

Is there a "nice room" in my dream that I don't let get dirty, use or touch?

_____

How do I ask for help when something is beyond my skill level to take care of?

_____

Do I believe that my needs will always be provided for?

_____

You have made it to the end of Part One! Now, we are clearer about what you are hauling along with you. Next, we will see how these beliefs can and will change when we "go big"... Let's go!

Part 2:

How to Go Big

We all have some vision that is even bigger than what we think we deserve, what is possible, or what is reasonable in this lifetime. When we enter that vision in reality, it can feel sacred – holy, even… it borders on being both exciting and terrifying – I call this big paradoxical state "excitifying."

Invitation: If you want to see images of the journey and how big the country was that we were in, please mosey on over to my website and check out my free workshop that includes pictures and a process to figure out what your big idea is right now.

1898 Miles

Independence Day

Bozeman, Montana

BIGGER THAN ME

"If there were a little more silence, if we all kept quiet…maybe we could understand something."

- Federico Fellini

I needed a bigger God. Somehow I always felt closer to God in the mountains. In college, I had taken an English class called "The Bible as Literature." One of the essay topics for the semester was called "High Places," and was a study of "The Sermon on the Mount" and other historical phenomena that took place on mountain tops. In my essay, I think I wrote something about mountains being closer to the supposed heavens (I identified as an agnostic at the time).

I recognized that my yearning for these higher places had been "Edging God Out," an acronym reminding me that perhaps "my ego" was trying to run the show here. Whenever I found myself taking responsibility for more than my share in the journey, I was trying to make my part bigger than God's. Sometimes it was hard for me to hear God, or find him in the details, preferring only to give Him credit in those foxhole moments. Now that I was in one, I found God speaking through my friends.

It turned out that the axle *was* running way too hot when we first checked an hour outside of Billings, and we weren't able to cool it. When we spat on it, it made a hissing sound, and we could tell it was sizzling, even though it was now almost pitch black. I'd been on the phone with USRider, trying to figure out exactly how bad it might be if the axle went off, and what our options were to prevent that. It didn't take me long to realize we had to get off the road and get the thing checked out – losing an axle on a mountain pass with all our loved ones in tow was absolutely not worth the risk.

The problem was that it was a national holiday, and every tow company we called was closed. Even USRider, our lifeline traveling with horses and trailers, was short staffed for a rescue arrangement at 9 pm on the 4th of July, although they were able to secure a place that could look at our trailer the next day. When I called them, the boss answered, "Don't take this the wrong way, ma'am, but my crew is verrrrry much off duty. We're drinking and setting off explosives. My property is no place for a group with young children and horses to be hanging out right now." I understood completely.

Next, I called my friend Veronica in Bozeman. She was expecting us to keep our horses with her for a few days and volunteered to drive an hour and a half over the mountain pass to bring them back for us. She was nursing a baby, sober, and seemed happy to help. I felt eternally grateful.

As we waited in a large pull-through parking lot downtown, the ground began to rattle. An earthquake of that magnitude didn't make sense, but my mind was grabbing at straws to figure out what was happening. Then I realized it was a train, and this was a commuter parking lot. In the dark, I could see the spotlight coming – a reminder that there was a light at the end of the tunnel, but that the journey can also be frightful to get there. I turned to calm the horses, who were also rattled by this development.

The train seemed to go on forever. In fact, it went on long

enough that the horses' heart rates returned to normal as they ate their hay from their hay bags, safe in their trailer home. When I stopped counting train cars, my friend arrived.

Veronica was a sight for sore eyes with her blonde hair pulled back under a ball cap, and her movie star lashes covering her smiling eyes. We had met on a plane flying from Jackson Hole to Chicago many years before. There was an irony in Veronica being behind the camera, because she could also easily be a model herself. She had been our wedding photographer, and became our friend. I gave her a huge hug – it's not every friend who will bail you out on a mountain pass at the end of a long summer holiday when your trailer breaks down.

"I don't know what I would have done without you!" I said again and again through happy tears. Then I took a look at her trailer. It was not what I expected.

"We call this the rust bucket," she joked. "It ain't much, but it's safe and it'll do." I was glad it was dark – I could see enough of it to know that under no other circumstances would I ever agree to have my horses loaded up in this thing. But these were strange times, and this rescue was bigger than me.

The bumper pull trailer had no dividers and was literally made of rusted metal. Our horses peered into it, incredulous that we were asking them to load up. I conveyed the message that this was the last step to green mountain pastures through my energy by touching them on the ground. They snorted, looking around at the city lights, gravel street, and train tracks beside us, where the train had finally disappeared, and recognized that anywhere else must be better than this. In one breath, all three squeezed in without any protest, the last one's butt hanging out the back until we snugged her in by swinging the door closed.

"One more hour, you guys, and you're home," I promised them. If only the same were true for us. While Veronica headed up the pass with our horses, we headed back out into the night to drop our trailer at the trailer company's parking lot. It was after midnight and no one was there – the party had long since ended. By the time we unhooked the trailer, it was 1 am.

Then we put the GPS into our phone to find Kitty's house. Veronica had space for our horses, but not for our humans or our dog. This would be the first time our crew had been separated like this. As we would arrive way past bedtime, Kitty gave me clear instructions about where our rooms were and asked us to come in quietly – they would hold the dogs upstairs so they didn't bark and see us in the morning. It would be after 2 am by the time we arrived. This had become a really big night.

In the end, even if we are on a mission with our families, under the same roof or in the same zip code, it's true that, in the words of Cher, "We all sleep alone." Of course, when we wake up, we get to face the music together, and every family has their own stuff going on, as I was about to be humbly reminded. Sometimes it feels like we are all vying for who has the biggest problem. When we do this, we forget to let God be the judge of what is big and allow His solutions to be bigger than our problems. We also forget the gift that friendship is and to let it unfold in every season, regardless of how big or little the reason.

As a professional photographer, Veronica had an eye for finding what she wanted, and they had found this incredible horse property in Billings where she'd opened up a second studio. We'd chatted the year before when I was first planning the trip, and she'd offered to host us in their pasture. It sounded picture perfect, and the next day, I would see it all. High on a hill, there was a small farmhouse and barn with the rust bucket parked outside. Our horses were grazing around the back of the barn happily – you could tell they felt that they had finally arrived – and had been "partying" in their own horsey way as well. Next to them, a 30-day-old foal grazed with his mother contentedly. Our horses also appeared to have been "reborn" in this place.

Veronica was always dressed to kill, and today was no exception as she walked towards us wearing a super stylish Navajo sweater wrap. She was clearly in her element. I asked to take a picture of her. When I raised my camera, I noticed the huge cross on the hill and pointed towards it. "That was when I knew," she explained, as she saw it catch my eye.

Then I also knew; I felt the faith of that sign and all I had walked through in my bones, like I had finally summited the peak I'd been climbing. It didn't really matter what any of us believed, as we'd all found our way in the end. That big cross on the hill reminded me that all of this had to be bigger than me, and that it was real, too – from my friends, to my family, to the mountains all around us. As Debbie Ford said, "It's not the thing itself, it's the meaning we ascribe to the thing." We had finally arrived in a single day, by going "nowhere."

WRITE, RECORD and SHARE

Use the space below to write a few sentences, or pull out your phone and record a short video. Share it with us on social media or through my website!

How BIG is your trust in God or "Good Orderly Direction" of the universe?

_____

What makes one friendship bigger than another?

_____

How do animals help you see what "heaven on earth" might look like?

_____

Describe "God's Country"

_____

What's "the BIG IDEA" behind your dream destination or desire?

_____

How will you know you have arrived?

_____

Great job beginning to unpack some of the big stuff! These are the thoughts and stories that appear brighter in our memories and minds. Let's continue to shine a light on them.

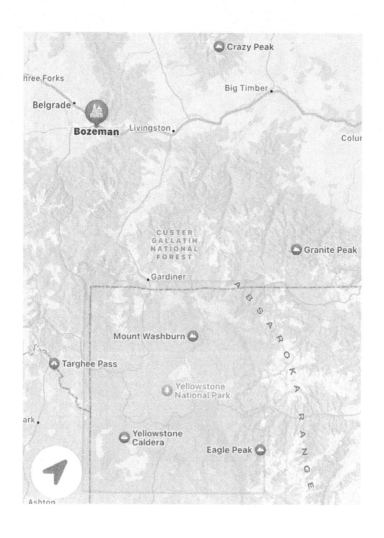

2255 Miles

July 5th

Suburbs of Bozeman

"KEEPING IT REAL"

"Childhood is the small town everyone came from."

-Garrison Keillor

Our first morning "out West," I'd like to say we woke up triumphant: *we'd made it*!! Honestly, I think we were still in shock from everything that had transpired to get us that far. We woke up slowly and groggily from the late night with the trailer, which we would go see later that day. The excitement to see our friends and finally be in the big mountains prompted us to "do something" to shake off the travel stress. Arriving wasn't enough – now it was time to "party." George and I had people to see, trailers to pick up, and things to do here to live another day.

We didn't party like we used to, of course. Neither of us drank anymore, which was a good thing. Of this crew of friends, only our wedding photographer knew us alcohol free, and sometimes my other friends missed drinking with me. The truth was, I'd found out who my friends were when I cleaned up my act, because some of them were just drinking buddies, and I wondered if this would be true with Kitty, who I had hardly seen since college, when we'd partied like rockstars. Under the influence of drugs and alcohol, I did bad things and bad things were done to me – it took me a long time to take responsibility for the cross I had to bear when it came to picking up just one (which always led to more than one). For me to keep it real, I was not sober curious, I had grown into being "sober positive."

My friends had also grown up. We wanted and needed

different things than the last time we had all come together when George and I got married. As moms, "party" meant taking an uninterrupted hike while Ruthie watched our children. Kitty and I started off our day this way, while George drove back over the hill to get the trailer from the mechanic who had fixed the axle. It felt great to stretch my legs and challenge my lungs with altitude. I missed the mountains dearly, and Kitty understood this. We had always been good hiking partners, and this was something we could still share – me as a tourist and Kitty as a local.

One thing I'd discovered at the University of Colorado was that there was a clear demarcation between "natives" and "transplants." Kitty was a chief supervisor on this lesson, having been born in Colorado herself and raised in Crested Butte. Although I'd been going to Colorado every year since I was eight, I was sensitive to the fact that "I wasn't from there." In high school, I returned to California, my official birth place, though I'd learned not to advertise that growing up in New Mexico. In college, I accepted that as long as you had a sense of humor about being a transplant and respected what it meant to actually be a native, you might be welcomed into the inner circle, but you'd never be "all the way in." In Jackson Hole, I learned that being a "local" was a coveted term earned after five or six seasons, or something like that. Only the locals knew the Hole meant a geographic depression surrounded by four mountain ranges. The same locals drove cars with bumper stickers that said, "Don't let the Hole lose its soul."

While in Jackson (aka Jackson Hole), I had a radio show called Car Mic (a pun on Karmic from Karma), and I decided to use it as a platform to engage our community in dialogue about being local. The question I asked of everyone I interviewed on the mountain or at the river's edge with my portable microphone was this: "What does it mean to be a local?" After a year of answers, I shifted my query to what I really wanted to know, and what seemed to draw out the best conversation by asking: "What does it mean to be real? And how do you *keep it real?*"

In hindsight, maybe it was the question that brought the best out in *me*. I had not come from humble beginnings, and I didn't like feeling like I needed to cover this up to be accepted. To be real meant to be okay with being myself, and also having humility about the fact that not everyone might be as financially or intellectually blessed as I had been. I had been blessed with a higher education, bought and paid for by my family, and I knew just how lucky I was and was often ashamed of my own luck. These things could either lead to my downfall or serve to be part of what made me real and, thereby, whole. Only when I released the desire to be something other than what I was would I be able to give the best part of myself as a local wherever I chose to be. Every day, in every way, I was always striving to be real.

Hiking was one of my favorite ways to keep it real. Kitty didn't understand why I'd moved to the city. Hiking through a cool mountain meadow filled with wildflowers, I had trouble explaining it. "We're where we are supposed to be right now," I said dryly, huffing and puffing my way through the motions. My heart wasn't in it. If I'd been listening to my own interview, I would have found this answer inauthentic.

So I dropped the rock and told her about how hard it was to be so close to so much family yet feel distant from them at the same time. Here we had come all this way to be near them, and while we were much closer to George's family, most of my family felt further and further away. We saw one another in passing, and at family events, but our connection lacked depth. I wished that my relationship with my relatives felt more real. I'd come to realize that some of my relatives had a tendency to flee when things got difficult, and here I was doing exactly that with our whole family in tow... if we hadn't left the cat, there was no telling whether or not we'd ever go back. Didn't we belong out here? Why had we ever left the mountains? What did we have to prove?

Family alone was not proving to be enough to feel fulfilled in the midwest. Moreover, putting the need to be fulfilled by our family's love, proximity, and approval was not a good recipe for anyone, and I could see that now. It was a dysfunctional setup, because we were close, but not that close, forever 20-35 minutes away from each other at any time. Being near family while we raised our family often felt like it was "in name only." There had to be a bigger purpose to our life there than just being close to family while we raised family. The quantity of family did not override the quality of connection that I craved. Instead, I felt I did not really belong and needed to find ways to prove that I did – to them, and to myself.

George's corporate job provided security, but it did not make our hearts sing by any means – it was a means to an end. Moreover, so many things in the midwest did not fit us that we had been morphing ourselves just to fit in, saying things like, "That's how you play the game." Kitty challenged me on these changes as we fell in step to our conversation. Beyond a passion for the outdoors and education, it appeared we had little in common now. My attempts to explain that I felt the way we won our house at auction and had two home births in it was divinely orchestrated was met with silence. She struggled with the "God stuff."

It was clear we did not see some things the same way, but we could hike. One step in front of the other, we made our way up and down the mountain and through the dry conversation and attempts to connect more deeply. I remembered Kitty saying when we turned back off a 14er summit because storm clouds were rolling in, "I have nothing to prove," and recognizing that much of my life I had been climbing mountains to prove something. The big one was proving that I was worthy of the wealth I had been born with, and I felt alone in this as I hiked with Kitty. I could see the pattern of needing approval not only from my family, but from my old friends, too… I was starting to feel the need only for a Higher Power's approval: but what did that really look like?

At the end of our workout, I offered to buy lunch as a thank you for Kitty hosting our whole family for three nights in her home. She agreed, and we went to a cute cafe to get takeout. While there, I was distracted by text messages to coordinate dinner at another local friend's house that night. Elizabeth (Liz) and I went to the same boarding school and became fast friends our freshman year, both of us coming to California from "random mountain states" that gave us a different perspective from many of our California classmates.

The party was going to go all day and all night, I could see. Kitty was game, and I found myself lost in thought as we headed back to regroup with George, Ruthie, and our children. Kitty's husband was out guiding a fishing trip and would not be back in time for dinner. George was on his way home with the trailer, which they had fixed and explained was a near miss on our lives. We would need to drop it at Veronica's place after the dinner party because it could not be stored in Kitty's neighborhood due to CC and Rs.

Kitty and Liz had laid eyes on each other at my wedding, but they were not fast friends. In anticipation of coming together at Liz's place, I was reminded just how vast our socio-economic differences were. While Liz was comfortable in my family's second home in Colorado, recognizing a financially kindred spirit, Kitty's experience was just the opposite, as she had felt more distant from me and had never gone back. My attempts at modestly excusing my family's wealth seemed to fall short with one friend and not be necessary with the other. In the presence of greater wealth than my own, I would find myself wishing for things they had, yet when I was the wealthier party, I had a pattern of beating myself up for it, then picking up the tab out of guilt. If I felt financially okay when others did not, I felt somehow responsible for this, and it was a bad pattern. The fact that I had not made the wealth myself only exacerbated that feeling, as it is popular in our culture to attack people for inherited wealth. I had done a lot of work not to loathe myself for this, instead embracing the gifts I was born with wholeheartedly for the highest good for all involved, and Liz understood this.

When I was single, I visited Liz's starter home in Denver where she became a mother. It was a respectable neighborhood with a great dog park nearby. I don't remember if she had a guest room or not, as I was just passing through on my drive from New Mexico to Wyoming and stopped for a quick bite to eat and a walk. A few years later, I visited her Bozeman home as a newlywed with George. That home was a big step up, with rooms for all three of their children and a guest room. We'd stayed with them, sharing the kids' bathroom and tub, which was filled with more fun bath toys than we knew what to do with. This time, she was now in another new home, one she could really grow into. It had a huge yard, acreage, and lots of space between neighbors. I could see that she was finally home: she had arrived, and I was happy for her. When I had given Kitty the address, she had made a comment about how this was one of the nicest neighborhoods in Bozeman, and I could feel the salt in the wound.

Having dinner there with Kitty, I could tell she might have felt somewhat "less than." I wished I could make this better for her. Kitty grew up around wealth in a ski town but had always compared herself to others. In college, we had been able to talk about this openly, but the divide seemed to have widened between us over the years, and we had not really touched upon it. She was a school teacher married to a fishing guide/teacher, and Liz not only came from wealth, like me, she was also married to a doctor who provided even more financial security, like my husband.

We had arrived early, and it was still hot enough for the kids to play in the sprinklers before dinner. Liz was a gracious hostess, keeping it real on every level with food and drinks appropriate for all ages, and our children naturally broke the ice by playing. I wondered if Liz, like me, felt somehow responsible for oversharing her gifts of affluence in mixed social settings. I focused my energy on the children and the gratitude I felt for all of us coming together, but the awkwardness of affluence was palpable. It wasn't about the money. Perhaps it was about all those missing links between us, so many years, so many stories we had not shared. Moreover, we had too much food, because there was one party missing – Veronica, who had RSVPed yes, then canceled because she was tired from her late night picking up our horses. After two hours of socializing and eating, we all called it a day.

WRITE, RECORD and SHARE

Use the space below to write a few sentences, or pull out your phone and record a short video. Share it with us on social media or through my website!

How, and with whom, will you celebrate your dream coming true?

_____

Who do you hike the mountain with and what do you talk about?

_____

Are you trying to prove something to someone? If yes, what is it and to whom? If not, why not?

_____

Have you ever had wealth create a separation among friends?

_____

Define "Big Money" in relation to your own economics:

_____

Have you been holding your family (or friends) up on a pedestal?

_____

There, there — you are starting to see how you differentiate between what seems big, what seems small, and why it matters to your dream. I'd love to have you share with me! This is where the big shifts really begin, as we see new possibilities for ourselves.

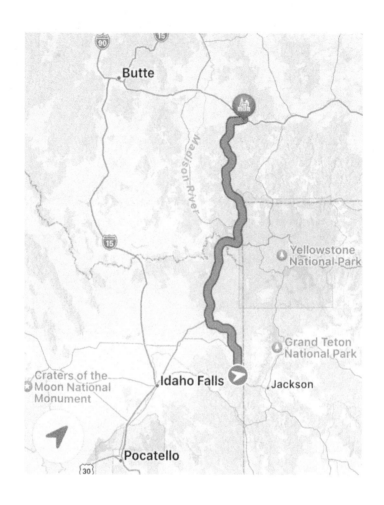

2596 Miles

July 6th

Driggs, Idaho

MY FAVORITE LANDLORD

"The right word may be effective, but no word was ever as effective as a rightly timed pause."

- Mark Twain

As we left Bozeman, Montana and headed back to Driggs, Idaho where we used to live, I found myself lost in thought, reflecting on my past. When I moved to the Tetons in 2007, I had two cats that I'd gotten as kittens in Chicago. They were siblings, and I named them after my favorite mountain towns, Jackson and Snowmass. It had been really hard finding places to live with pets, and I'd made some bad decisions, especially in transition, like trying to camp outside with my cats one summer in Wilson, Wyoming. Usually, I'd get them into a friend's apartment or house while I camped, when there wasn't room for a human, but I'd run out of offers and decided to return to nature with them. I had no idea how seriously nature was going to take me up on my offer.

After all, I'd be there to protect them and keep watch. This had been going well for about a month, and I felt that perhaps it was a new beginning. My current caretaking gig had allowed us to camp out by their pasture, and my cats had seemed happy to be outside all the time. We were sleeping on top of a large stack of hay bales, creating a 20-foot climb and lookout from any predators, under the light of the full moon. Snowmass was nestled into the downy softness by my head. Jackson cuddled up with me in my sleeping bag, crawling under to lay by my stomach intermittently, then left to hunt indefinitely. That was the last I saw of her.

It took a few days for me to find her body. I knew it was her from a distance, or what was left of her anyway. She had been taken out by some larger beast and devoured. In my quest for meaning in her disappearance, I learned that we were camping on Native American hunting grounds, and that the spirits and animals never rested easy here... now that I'd found myself in this horrible predicament, the only thing left to make peace and seek shelter for those still living. I buried her on the spot and held a ceremony for her there, returning the next day only to find that the animal had dug her remains up for a second helping. It was more than I could bear. I hated myself and gave her brother, Snowmass, away to a more reliable friend with an actual home and another cat companion of his own.

There was no excuse for my behavior. My recklessness of 2008 had led to the death of my beloved cat, and I had learned my lesson. If I was going to be a parent to animals, I needed a home, not just where the buffalo roam, but one with a reliable shelter for safety from predators, and spirits. Moreover, I needed animals who could safely come with me, so I started migrating towards horses and dogs exclusively. In the end, this was naive, for any domestic animal is potential prey in the wild west. Even me. My nomadic lifestyle and poor judgment were connected to my drinking, and that began to change when I sobered up in the spring of 2009. Things started to fall into place with a dream home for my animals and me shortly thereafter.

The problem, two years later, was my growing herd and responsibilities. I now had another cat, a dog, *and* a horse, alongside a brick-and-mortar business that anchored me to Idaho.

Moreover, I had met George, aka "the one," and needed to think about a space that would fit all of us, wherever we were going.

Lost in thought, I saw a woman I'd never met walk into my fitness club. She was petite, but tough – with the kind of grit, confidence, and joy that one sees only in long-term locals, the ones entirely at home on the planet. Introducing herself as Evie, she immediately took the reins and informed me that she was interested in starting up a membership through our silver sneakers program, but she didn't want to start just yet.

"Why wait?" I probed, gently reaching across the spiritual sales conversation to take the reins back and guide her into membership, as I had been trained to do. "Exercise is good for whatever ails ya! Let's get you started today!" I said cheerfully.

She smiled and replied, "No, not yet – I have to find a renter for my place first. Nice place – do you know anyone looking for a 2 bedroom apartment in Driggs?"

"Funny you ask, because that is just what I'm looking for! Do you take horses?" I asked, half joking.

Without skipping a beat, she said, "I have three. How many do you have?"

On my lunch break, I went and looked at her place. This duplex was a huge step up for me. Not only was it beautiful, designed by her partner who was an architect, it was walking distance to work, and to where my horse would be with her herd (horses are herd animals after all, so I knew he would love this). Moreover, the 20-acre pasture had a seasonal mountain stream nestled in an aspen grove, with plenty of shelter to get out of the storm as needed. This cool new landlady brought it all together and made me an offer I could not refuse, letting me board my horse for $100/month if I'd support her caretaker during the winter months when she was in Arizona. It was a win-win for all of us.

Our actual friendship emerged slowly. I'd been living on her property for almost 365 days before we finally went on a trail ride together, in part because she spent 6 months of every year in Arizona. Evie was in her late 80s and could keep up with the best of them. We rode a steep trail with a friend of hers up, up, up into the fall colors of the Teton range. It was the first and last time I ever saw her ride. Mostly, she liked to be with her horses on the ground and seemed happiest "back at the ranch." Perhaps her riding days, like her flying days, were mostly behind her.

Somewhere along the way, I met her amazing partner and learned more about their adventures together. When first courting, they had sailed for a month off the coast of San Francisco. Evie had worked as a flight attendant, but also as a wrangler and guide taking dudes horse-packing into the wilderness. I never got to put together the full story, but I identified with her many trades, and the difficulty in keeping track of them, because that had been the story of my life, too. She had deep roots in the Tetons, but her traveling spirit gave them breadth.

In part, I knew I was going to see her and everyone else in person. She had to be in her 90s now, and we had left before she got back from Arizona in the spring of 2015, so we never got to say goodbye. I was also going to say hello, of course, and to continue to scratch the surface of the friend I always hoped to get to know at a deeper level. But sometimes when you go the distance to meet someone else, thinking you'll learn more about them, you don't find them. Instead, you find yourself.

WRITE, RECORD and SHARE

Use the space below to write a few sentences, or pull out your phone and record a short video. Share it with us on social media or through my website!

What does the ultimate version of yourself feel like?

_____

What exercise would feel big for you right now?

_____

If you could imagine the biggest and best home for you and your animals, what would it look like?

_____

Have you ever had a big breakthrough while going through the motions at a job?

_____

What big dark secret in your past is holding you back?

_____

What would healing from this secret look like?

_____

Are you a match for the kinds of animals you are responsible for (or want to be) in your life?

_____

Now we go deep and wide to explore what is big. So often the projection of what is "big" in our present or future comes from experiences in the past. Keep thinking bigger – the impossible IS possible somewhere, somehow…

2707 Miles

July 6th

Darby Canyon, Idaho

KEEP UP RIDERS

"Dancing is like a shower: one wrong turn and you're in hot water!"

- Mad Magazine

George and I married in the summer of 2012 at The Chapel of Transfiguration in Grand Teton National Park. This small chapel was built for all the dude ranches in the area back in the 1920s. It is essentially a log cabin in the middle of a corral with a huge window at the back of it framing the Grand Teton Range. It was everything we wanted it to be and more, followed by a party on top of a hill where all our friends toasted us. I think it was Kitty who said, "Well, Cat – and George, I don't really know you, but from what I've heard everyone else say and what I know about Cat – it looks like you've finally found your match in someone who can keep up!!" Her toast was well received... because it was all true.

George and I had always had a tendency to chase adventure off the cliff itself, then find ourselves screaming at each other as we fell into whatever stop sign was necessary to land us, be it a meal or campsite or night itself. Exhausted, we would kiss and make up before doing it all again. We are both crazy about each other and our zest for adventure. Given all the breakdowns and changes due to the weather, we would only have one day together in Teton Valley, so we planned to pack it in and "go big," as usual.

First, we said our goodbyes to our Montana posse, then

made our way around Yellowstone into Idaho. Ruthie was trained up now and drove a few hours south from West Yellowstone to Driggs. At one point, she rounded a blind curve to see a large red mound in the middle of the road. There was barely enough space to get around it using the shoulder without falling, but she did it seamlessly, knowing there definitely wasn't space to brake safely with such a heavy load behind us.

After we passed it, all of us caught our breath, looking back in the rear view to acknowledge that it was a kayak. Half an hour later, a large truck pulled out to pass another vehicle and headed straight for us in the oncoming lane, down a hill, no less. "What the…?" George said in the front passenger seat, but Ruthie said nothing, and again pulled to the right to safely dodge the potential accident, by a hair's length. Then she let out a huge sigh, saying, "Thank you, Jesus."

We stopped an hour later at the Frost Top, and I bought Ruthie an ice cream soda and a T-shirt, telling her she had "earned her stripes" today and applauding her for how safely she had navigated what could have been a disaster. Ruthie had never driven a horse trailer until a few days before, when we had begun teaching her how to feather the brakes and make wide turns with the trailer empty at our first stop in South Dakota. Today had been her first real mountain driving challenge, and she had passed it in flying covers with two bonus tests thrown in. Over and over, she would prove to have brought along some of her own angels to save us, and demons to slay.

When we pulled into Evie's pasture, I could feel the horses let out a big sigh of relief as well. They'd slept in five different pastures and paddocks over the last ten days, and Jet and Solita knew they were finally home in their original big pasture. Of the three, Tiki was the only horse who had never been here, and I wondered if they were telling her, energetically, that this was the place where they used to live, and that they had been praying we were going back to.

Evie was a sight for sore eyes, her tiny 90-year-old frame bounding through the grass to meet us! She gave us all huge hugs, then helped us lead Solita, who she'd always had a soft spot for, back into a holding pen. Solita was impossible to catch on the 20 acres when she wanted to be, so we knew we would have to separate our herd from her herd if we wanted to plan on taking a ride later, and not a two-hour "catching lesson."

After getting the horses situated, we took our sleeping children to the other home where we would be sleeping. Evie had an amazing guest loft above the tack barn, but it wasn't enough for all of us, and our trailer only had one bed in it, so we decided to divide and conquer. George and I would sleep in the guest loft with Dani, who was still nursing, and keep an eye on the horses, while Ruthie would stay at Tooty and Joe's house four miles away. It was going to be a little bit annoying not all being together, but we would manage.

The girls were delighted by the old cabin that was set back against the mountain down the road where I found my first horse tribe in Idaho. Tooty and Joe were long-time hippies who also had professional careers as therapists. Ironically, Joe and I had been competitors, as he also owned a gym, but in the end, we had sold them some of our equipment when we closed our fitness club and had finally become friends. My knee injury had been partly to thank for that, as it brought me into physical therapy with Tooty after years of trying to rehab with other therapists. As the saying goes, "When the student is ready, the teacher will appear."

I'd been hot-tubbing at their place, but we had never stayed there. Sometimes I wonder how serious people are when they say, "Come stay with us." Of course, you find out when you cash in. Tooty and Joe turned out to be the real article, delighting in our children, while also developing a real friendship with Ruthie. She later went back to visit them on her own with her husband when they invited her back also – ever the spirit of Western hospitality.

Ruthie had never met anyone "like them," she later confided, meaning "non-Christians" who behaved like Christians. The way they served us, housed us, clothed us, and loved us without asking for anything in return was truly spiritual, maybe even biblical, if that's how you look at things. "I can't believe they're not Christians," she said.

"Keep up!" I thought, "Don't you know that not every good person on the planet is also a self-proclaimed Christian? There are great people, Godly people, who also don't believe in God, our God or another's, who are doing amazing things for and with 'God's people.'" Sometimes this contradiction of reality irritates me. I often thought of Gandhi's famous quote, "I like your Christ, but I do not like your Christians." At the end of the day, anyone can practice a pure message of truth and love, regardless of their religious ideation.

I could see that this was going to be an amazing awakening for her in her own beliefs. Meanwhile, it was time for her to get the girls settled while George and I went out for a quick ride and dinner – our first "date night" since the trip had started would also be our only night together in the Tetons, since George was leaving the next day. After getting everyone's toys, books, toiletries, clothes, and beds set up, we took a quick nap to nurse and chill before leaving for a sunset ride.

It was already 5 pm, and we realized we were starving. We needed to eat, then ride, and had already decided on our favorite restaurant, Teton Thai, which was walking distance from Evie's duplex at the far end of the pasture where we used to live. By the time we were done eating, it was getting late, but this didn't stop us, as usual.

The horses seemed a little annoyed that they were getting loaded up again after having already been in the trailer for 3 hours that morning and finally arriving home to the best pasture ever, but they complied. We took Tiki along, too, to lead her up and down the mountain trails to get her feet under her, since we knew she had never seen anything like this, having been born and raised in the midwest for the first 5 years of her life. Our horses would be familiar with the Aspen Trail, as it was an old favorite that we used to ride, and close to where Ruthie was babysitting the girls so we could easily pick Dani up after.

I took a picture of George mounting his horse as we left the trailer, noting that it was literally almost sunset already. "They know the trail," we reasoned with each other, as we rode up the mountain. By the time we got to the outlook 30 minutes later, we realized that the 45 minutes of dusk-light was up. We decided to take a shortcut down a ravine to get back to the trailer before it was totally pitch black. Of course, we hadn't ridden this trail in years, since we'd moved away, and apparently, no one else was using this shortcut anymore. By the time we realized how overgrown it was, we were too far in to turn around, and it was very dark.

"This is very us," we joked, still in good spirits but surfing on the edge of our old ways. It was one thing to behave this way when we didn't have children, but it was something else entirely now that we did have kids. What if something happened to us? Luckily, our horses seemed to feel the same way about getting back to their old herd and greener pastures. Once Solita got us safely off the hill, George switched mounts mid-stride without letting his feet touch the ground to give her a break and let Tiki have some weight on the flat gravel road back to the trailer.

As we made our way in the dark, I marveled at this amazing horseman who had shown up after we said our vows. George had been on a horse only twice before we got married – and the second time was the week before our wedding, when he fell off due to a half blind horse and an unfortunate tree branch which stuck her in the ribs on a trail ride with my friend Glenda. The thing that mattered most was that he got back on, and kept getting back on with me after that. This was the grit we needed for marriage, and I knew we'd be riding into the sunset and through the darkness for eternity together with it. After all, we'd finally found a partner in one another who could keep up.

WRITE, RECORD and SHARE

Use the space below to write a few sentences, or pull out your phone and record a short video. Share it with us on social media or through my website!

What does a Godly person or experience feel like?

_____

Who do you like to play in the dark with?

_____

Have you found your adventure match?

_____

What would a big relationship upgrade look like for you?

_____

When you fall off the horse, how do you get back on?

_____

Describe the feeling of being with a partner or group that can keep up, and shares, your big dream:

_____

Reach out to your loved ones now, and share some big words of gratitude for all you have been through. If it is time, share with them what you dream of next, and make the big ask if you want them to join you! After all, even our loved ones aren't mind readers — and neither am I. Tell me more...

Mile 2777

July 7th

Home Alone in the Tetons

THE HOLEY POTTY

"We can't choose the music that life gives us, but we can choose how to dance to it."

- Unknown

Everyone has to deal with poop in life. It's not pretty, but it's a fact. What we do with it and how that affects others is where the real legacy comes in. George having a job he had to leave us for felt kind of like poop, and that got me thinking about it. When you are changing diapers a lot and caring for animals, caring for poop is just a way of life!

On the river, when I was a river guide, we practiced "leaving no trace" to preserve the precious water that carries us, cleans us, and soothes our ears and souls for days on end by packing all of our waste out, along with trash and everything else. The portable toilet used on overnight rafting trips is technically an army ammo can made of steel, about 8 by 15 inches and a foot and a half deep. On top, we fasten a normal-looking toilet seat with a lid and take turns finding a desirable and private view for the loo to be placed at each campsite. River guides affectionately dub this box the "groover" because, in the old days, it didn't have a seat and would leave grooves on your bum. But nowadays, we joked that it was because you felt so groovy after you were done. One thing hadn't changed in all those years, and that was the self-sufficiency of it all: "You pack it in, you pack it out."

The next best thing to a groover, in my mind, was a composting toilet, and that was exactly what my friends had in the cabin they'd built at the base of the hill where we were staying. Downstairs, in a backroom of the basement, there was an enormous vaulted mechanism that processed the family's doo-doo into organic matter. Upstairs, the toilets had gaping holes two or three stories high, like inverted skyscrapers, which were a bit of a hazard with the little ones. Of course, they were oblivious to the potential hazard; their primary concern was scooping the wood chips – one for pee and two for poo – into this incredible machine of a "toilet that didn't flush."

I realized that this was the next best thing to actually camping with them at these ages and loved the opportunity for teaching that it provided. We brought our own small folding stepladders to reach the sinks and settled into living this cozy cabin life with our hosts. They led busy lives and were gone a lot, which gave us ample opportunity to chill and catch up with some of my other old friends.

Catching up with old friends was great, and Ruthie was amazing to work with, but it did not replace the feeling of incompleteness I felt without George being there. Despite having Ruthie and my friends around to share the load of childcare, doggy duty, and horse needs, I still felt the onus and responsibility of being a single parent. I was deeply humbled by this and reminded of the importance of working it out and staying together, especially when things started to smell.

Like all marriages, we have a healthy banter that sometimes turns into a bicker, and the stress of managing young children, horses, a dog, a nanny, our old community, breakdowns, and the like had definitely brought us to the breaking point a few times as we tried to keep up with the new normal. No doubt, we had brought on this load by overindulging in adventure, and there was no telling how big a dump or toll it would take on us later. But distance clearly made the heart grow fonder and helped us see just how beautiful and deep what we had was.

Marriage had broken my spirit of being single to regrow as a partner in the same way that motherhood had cracked me open wide again to become a parent. I was no longer the same person I had been when I was single; then again, after I had carried two pregnancies to term and nursed my babes, I myself was different – I thought differently, and I felt things differently. We were close as a family, and some of that closeness had come out of the healing necessary after a breakdown, when you rebuild together as something new.

The miracle of this time apart was that I could see myself in a new light juxtaposed against the old town I'd moved to as a single girl in my twenties. Jackson Hole hadn't changed much – the seasonal traffic and jobs were still evident, but I had changed. I wasn't looking for trouble anymore. Now I was looking for adventures and tools to carry my children into the wilderness well. I went to the saddle shop in search of a kid's saddle with Grace. While there, George called us from Abu Dhabi. We Facetimed as we walked around, Grace picking up everything that was pink: halter, brush, boots, and a pink glow in the dark lariat just her size for roping fake cattle.

John, the owner of the saddle shop, who had known me when I drove my Zebra Striped art car and worked for a wealthy woman from whom I purchased Jet, chuckled to see me now. "I feel like I'm coming back as one of the rich people," I said, pinching myself as he helped me load the kid's saddle into the bed of the truck and we caught up a bit on life. It was hard to be honest, to be this new me – the mother, horse road trip adventure leader, and corporate housewife. Some part of me still just felt like that little turd of a ski girl thinking about where she'd be packing groovers in the next season.

Now my life revolved around supporting my husband when he had to travel for work and taking care of our children and animals without him there. It was such a strange dichotomy. Some part of it stunk – it didn't make sense in that down-to-earth way I was looking for. But another part of it was absolutely glorious. I felt like an outlaw in my own suburban life. I was a rebel with a cause: to bring the western way of life to those far from it in the midwest and still remain true to the midwestern value of keeping the family together.

Here we were, making it happen in our way – dealing with the poop of life, not as we would have it, but as it was. In this new chapter of life, I was embracing my role, even when it felt like it sucked, because we were not all together and I wanted us to be. Once again, I felt the protection and spirit of our higher power playing through the dynamic of this time apart. Like sleeping, and using the loo, I knew that this was something I had to do on my own.

WRITE, RECORD and SHARE

Use the space below to write a few sentences, or pull out your phone and record a short video. Share it with us on social media or through my website!

How do you deal with life on life's terms?

_____

When it comes to poop, how do you manage it for yourself, your children, and your animals?

_____

Is there a big shift you can make around the things you have to do on a daily basis to love them more?

_____

When you are separated from your loved ones, and feel a big loss, how do you stay connected?

_____

Are you honest with others about who you are and how you've changed, or do "you say it best when you say nothing at all?"

_____

Sometimes what we really need is help making things "right sized." Our belief that something is bigger than or smaller than it is can often leave little room for grace. As we turn the page on this chapter, let's embrace all we are becoming!

Mile 2859

July 9th-10th

More Trails in Idaho

"OUR ESSENTIAL NATURE"

"Colors are the smiles of nature."

- Leigh Hunt

Two days after George left, I had my first trail ride scheduled with Shannon. We did a lot of riding together right before I moved, because I was between jobs and she needed a gelding, which I had, as a riding partner for her young mare at that time. Things had not changed in regard to sex; the day before our ride, she called and clarified that my mares were not welcome on a ride with her mare – it would have to be Jet, my gelding, who her mare had ridden with before, because she hadn't gotten her out much and she knew she would be really fussy with another mare's energy. There is a one-word saying among some horse people, and it goes like this: "marrrrrrrrres" or "mare-ish" with a knowing twinkle in the eye. Let's just say that their hormones can make them quite "a piece of work," and our own mares were no exception to the rule.

I'd never owned a mare myself until Solita, and when she went into "season" with us, I learned just how obnoxious a mare can be. One time, she began dancing and squirting, let's just call them "sexual juices" over a fence at an onlooking herd when George and I took a ride in the neighborhood. These hormones likely also contributed to her being so difficult to catch at times. Her most serious offense, of course, was kicking.

The last ride George and I took with Barbie before she moved to Taos, Solita turned and began kicking her mare aggressively without any warning only seconds after they touched noses in greeting. It happened so fast that none of us knew what hit us until it was over. I was reminded that you cannot trust a mare in heat and to look for the signs – an ounce of prevention is better than a pound of cure. Luckily, everyone was ok.

When I was eight months pregnant, she kicked me in the stomach. It was not the first time she had lashed out at me, but now I said I would not take care of her anymore, because it wasn't safe, and we sent her away to a friend's ranch for half a year. She'd come back with a breathing condition called heaves, which also made her feeding regime more difficult with added medicine. They say that grief is connected to lungs, and I wondered if she was grieving being away from George as he transitioned into fatherhood. Needless to say, she was always on thin ice with me, but a saint with George, and we joked that she was like "the other woman," me being her only competition with "her" man. She still had a home because she proved to be safe with our small children thus far, and, of course, George loved her very much, especially being his first horse.

Our second mare, Tiki, was a very easy keeper by comparison. I actually couldn't tell when she was or was not in heat, and that was a good sign. She was the bottom of the herd in terms of a pecking order, but on this trip, she was about to emerge as a strong leader whose hormones were in check. Regardless of her being mellow, it was often the energy that a mare brought up in the other mare that was the problem. Therefore, I was happy to surrender to my friend's wishes, and she was not done outlining them. "I'm also a bit of a control freak," she reminded me, "so I'd like to drive my own trailer if you don't mind."

"No big deal!" I chuckled. "I've driven a few thousand miles in

112

the past week, and I'd love the break from all that hauling responsibility."

The next thing we had to figure out was where we were going to go. It was a big snowpack year, which meant a lot of the high country still hadn't thawed, even in mid July, so we would need to pick lower trails in the valley. We agreed to hit up South Leigh, the first place we had ever ridden together, which offered a nice flat loop with several creek crossings and meadows full of wildflowers – we hoped. This was going to be a big event either way, just to get out, but God had even bigger ideas in store for us.

That morning, I woke up with Dani in the guest loft. Until this trip, I'd never been inside it and seen the curious decorations on the walls and interior. There was a classic old Western saddle, complete with a matching bridle and Navajo saddle pad hanging over a banister that separated the bed(room) from the living room. This was a big beautiful vision for a westerner like me, with a loft apartment above a working barn. My thirst for the wild west, horses, and nature was and is, to this day, insatiable. Big mountains, big plans, and big storms were part of that.

Grace, Dani, and I were looking out the barn loft window at the thunder clouds rolling in and listening to the thunder and rain that had been coming and going since the wee hours. I'd given Ruthie the night off by sleeping with both children in the loft, and she was in communication with me to come get them before I began saddling up. Then my phone made a strange ping sound. It was an alert for "severe thunderstorms in the area."

At that moment, I heard a gigantic crack, and it was as though the floodgates had opened, as it began to pour. I looked at my phone's weather forecast. It appeared that the rain would be going on and off throughout the morning but never very heavily. Mostly it was the thunder and lightning we needed to consider, as the heaviest rain would be over in about half an hour.

With the rain droning on in the background, I checked a local weather forecaster I follow online and was annoyed to see this suggestion: "Outdoor activities that can be avoided should be, seek shelter and alter plans." Unfortunately, this was the only day we had to do this. I called my riding partner to discuss.

Shannon was looking at the same weather forecast and battling the same internal dialogue about whether or not to go. We agreed that we could always ride out and back in that first half if it got nasty. By the time we were 40 minutes out, it was just as fast to keep going all the way around the whole loop, (or so we thought). Ruthie came to get the kids, we loaded up the horses and headed down the road, just like old times.

At the trailhead, we met some acquaintances coming off the trail. It was only 10 am, so they must have started pretty early, and they had clearly gotten stuck in the worst of it. Their horses had black mud all the way up past their bellies, and they explained that the back half of the trail was deeply flooded and bogged in. It was shocking to see this contrast on such large mammals: they looked like strawberries dipped in extra dark chocolate. "Don't do the whole loop," they pleaded. "It was really scary – our horses could have broken legs in there – we had no idea until it was too late." Then they told us they had actually started around 6 or 7 am, trying to get in and out before the high point of the storm, but the delays due to the unkempt trail conditions had landed them in the eye of it.

Sobered by this visual warning, we saddled up and headed out, gingerly. It began raining about twenty minutes into our ride, and we put on our slickers. When the rain got heavy, we pulled into a huddle of trees, and it began to hail down. We talked between bursts about our lives, catching up on what had changed and what had stayed the same.

Shannon told me about her aging mother and her struggles managing her needs alongside the conversation about that with her siblings. It sounded nearly identical to my parents, aunts, uncles, and grandparents. This was when I realized we are all really in the same story, just "walking each other home." It's only our egos that separate us.

Somehow this epiphany seemed bigger than it was, like this giant storm we had decided to ride into the middle of, against all odds and weather warnings. We needed each other to talk and stand in the rain, witnessing one another's journey through story. As our horses gently stood in solidarity together with us, waiting out the rush of water pouring down from the sky, I also saw that their grace and comfort with one another mirrored ours. We were completely present to each other, and to our mutual experience of all things seen and unseen, felt and unfelt. Throughout our time together, I felt that we were one.

A few days later, my friend Daisy had reached out to go for a ride. I put her on Solita, and we went up Horseshoe Canyon, an easy ride and one of my very favorites. Poor Solita had given her the run around, riding her off trail and making it really difficult for us to carry on much of a conversation, as I was spending most of the time giving Daisy a lesson about how to keep her on the trail. Despite her efforts to follow my directions, which were commendable, Solita had made up her mind to ride her own trail in typical mare-ish fashion.

Truthfully, working with mares has taught me a lot about paying attention to my own hormones and working with other women as well. Ironically, when Daisy and I first met, I had dubbed her "the competition." She was a little bit older than me but a total cougar. Her dirty blonde hair hung in ringlets, and she had the perfect amount of natural makeup on to highlight her real beauty. Eventually, we became fast friends, probably because we were both trailblazers, and we learned to collaborate, reading one another's energy as a gift, not a hindrance.

Needless to say, we hadn't made it very far down the trail before we decided to call it a day and head back to spend the rest of our time together with Ruthie and the kiddies at the trailhead. Sometimes women, like mares, just need to chill out together, regardless of the weather, because there is something going on inside of us that passes between us. Like the soil of the earth that cracks dry, then runs wet, we move in hormonal cycles, as is our innate nature. Nursing my daughters and traveling with my female friends in this way, I felt closer than ever to my own essence and understanding of the world and its rhythms.

WRITE, RECORD and SHARE

Use the space below to write a few sentences, or pull out your phone and record a short video. Share it with us on social media or through my website!

Are you working with your hormones?

_____

How big do your monthly cycles feel to you?

_____

Do you ride into the eye of the storm?

_____

Has your relationship with your hormones changed?

_____

When you meet your hormonal mirror, are you kicking them, or is it a match made in heaven?

_____

What does co-regulating your hormones look like for you?

_____

Learning to work with my hormones was really big for me — in fact, it completely changed my life. If you have not tapped in to this work, please reach out. It is both fascinating and life altering!

Mile 2946

July 13th

Teton Canyon, Wyoming

BREATHE IN THE MOUNTAINS

"After all, Ginger Rogers did everything that Fred Astaire did. She just did it backwards and in high heels."

– Ann Richards

There was no way I was going to be able to see everyone that I knew, or had known, in Teton Valley, having lived there for close to a decade. Instead of worrying about who I did or did not get to see, and where I did and did not get to ride, and with whom, I just let things unfold naturally, trusting that I would see and ride with exactly who I was supposed to. In recovery rooms, I've heard many sayings that help me keep my head above water. "More will be revealed" is an all-time favorite of mine, along with "you are exactly where you are supposed to be" and "who is meant to be there, will be" or "who you see here and what you hear here, let it stay here." These thoughts were my mantras as my social calendar filled up.

I had given up the idea of long rides long before this trip got started, in part because I was still nursing and couldn't be away from my baby for more than 4-6 hours without pumping, and in part because it was obvious that the road trip itself was going to be the ride, with little excess energy left for actual riding on the part of myself, my partner or our horses. We'd cherry-picked the only ride we would get to do together on our first night in town before George had left, and now I had space for only a few more rides. I knew that I had to make it out for at least one ride with my old neighbor, Glenda – why not make it my favorite trail of all time?

Glenda was a very talented rider, but between caring for a herd of nearly 10 horses and 5 dogs all by herself, along with working a full-time job to pay for them, it was no wonder that she didn't get out to ride much. When she did, she went all in, and I loved her stories about packing the whole herd into the backcountry for 3-6 days at a time, often alone, except for the animals. She was and is to this day one of the most incredible people I know.

That morning, I went to get my nails done, sort of a strange choice given my backcountry nature and limited time in the valley, but I had a few reasons for this. First of all, I'd started getting my nails done when I was on crutches as a result of my knee injury in our first year of marriage, and had fallen in love with these fun nail stamps they had at this salon. Second, it was through that salon that we found out about Solita from the nail tech (careful what you ask for – she was "for sale on Facebook!"). Third, I had put on this bright green shellac (green means GO!) before we left home, and it was nearing the three-week mark and needed to be taken off with straight acetone in a salon so my nails wouldn't rot – something I didn't know how to do myself, oddly enough.

Even still, for those who know me, getting my nails done may sometimes seem out of character, and when Glenda saw them, I knew she would tease me for it. Although we were on the other side of the 4th of July, I chose to decorate my nails with a red, white, and blue theme, complete with horseshoes, stripes, stars, and other cowgirl stamps to complete "the look." After all, it was a free country, and a trip like this wouldn't be possible without our freedom. I wanted to keep my patriotism going through this marathon of the middle.

First, I needed coffee, so I stopped at my favorite coffee shop, Pendl's, to write and get caffeinated. I sat down at an outdoor table, listening to the birds chirp, and then Teresa, another local friend, called. I saw Glenda calling me while I was in the middle of figuring out how to meet up with this other friend, so I declined the call, deciding I would call her back after. Teresa and I were chatting about how I'd just gotten my nails done and a few other things when I heard someone behind me saying, "Yeah, she drove her horses and kids all the way out here from Chicago to get her nails done!!"

Then I turned around to see Glenda sitting there with her partner and another gentleman. We laughed so hard, I nearly peed myself – actually, I probably really did pee myself – that's what happens after two kids. I ended my phone call and "got present" with my riding buddy and her friends in the real space that we found ourselves in.

The man I didn't know was a horse chiropractor from somewhere in distant Wyoming. Glenda had put him up for a few nights while he did business in the area in exchange for treating her horses. "I bet my horses would love to meet you," I said. He agreed, but a few days later, when I called him, he had already left.

The first time Glenda and I went out for a ride, Jet was still pretty young, and I had warned her that he had a tendency to buck, especially when loping with a group. As we went cantering up a road, he began bucking like a wild thing, and she reached over and took him by the bit. It was one of the only times I've ever had someone reach out to help me on a horse of my own like this, and I was truly touched by the kind gesture.

I was honored to have her ride and get to know the newest member of our herd, Tiki. She was worth her weight in gold and also happened to be a palomino, nicknamed "the Barbie horse." When my neighbor had called me asking if I was interested in a great kids' horse, my first thought thad been, "I need another horse like a hole in the head," but for some reason, I said, "Yes, I am," and it had been one of the best decisions I'd ever made for our family. Tiki was young, of course, only about 5 years old when we got her, which made her closer to 7 now, and she had a long way to go before a child could ride her without an adult companion. Moreover, she was very attached to being with other horses, and I wondered how this trip and, in particular, this trail ride up Teton Canyon would go with her.

Because I'd been away from Dani engaging in self-care and other "shenanigans" all morning, our time to ride was running short. By the time we hit the trail, we would only have about two hours to ride. At the 60-minute mark, I could feel my breasts bulging against the button-down shirt I was wearing, and I told Glenda we would need to turn back.

"Cat," she said, pulling Tiki up beside me, "you have come all this way. Couldn't you just take a minute to stop and breathe in the mountains?" That's when it hit me – the truth of the monstrosity of the task I had set out to do, and how, in doing so, I had forgotten about what really matters: finding time to breathe it all in and be present. After all, if you're not breathing, you are not present, and how you are breathing and showing up changes your presence. I took a deep breath and just appreciated that moment on Jet, with Chadeaux, my friend on Tiki, and her dogs all around us doing the same thing. It was ahhhhh-some. I could finally breathe it all in.

WRITE, RECORD and SHARE

Use the space below to write a few sentences, or pull out your phone and record a short video. Share it with us on social media or through my website!

When was the last time you took a really big breath?

_____

The little things are the big things: what little things are you missing out on right now?

_____

Are you responsible for how others perceive you?

_____

If I commit to take a really big journey that takes everything I've got, how will I remember to pause and take in the moment?

_____

What mantras keep me grounded when faced with something that feels BIG?

_____

Go embrace a little thing – enjoy a breath of fresh air, pet your cat, embrace your children, savor an ice cream cone. Life happens not just in the big moments, but in the little ones. Please reach out and share your moment with us!

Mile 3277

July 16th

Flaming Gorge, Utah

THE DESERT MEDICINE

"In a society that worships love, freedom and beauty, dance is sacred. It is a prayer for the future, a remembrance of the past and a joyful exclamation of thanks for the present."

– Amelia Atwater-Rhodes

After ten days in our old stomping grounds, it was time to head south towards where George would meet us in a few days' time. The drive was uneventful. We watched the landscape change from mountains to flatlands entering Utah, and, crossing over I-80, to desert. I'd grown up in the southwest, but I never felt fully at home there. Perhaps because my formative years were in Washington state, near a snow-covered mountain, apple orchards, and luscious pine trees in a town of about 20,000 people – the same size as Jackson Hole, Wyoming, I later realized.

Needless to say, we were clearly leaving my comfort zone – my happy place. To shake the feelings of loss, I focused on the place where we were headed in the middle of the Flaming Gorge desert and practiced being present to what was all around me. The colors of the rock and dirt were yellow, orange, and red now, with little shrubs and even less greenery dotting the landscape. This was a place where rain was both welcomed and shamed, as the parched earth couldn't soak it up fast enough, seeming to sing as it did, and thunderstorms often led to flash floods in the arroyos. I'd grown up respecting the sudden changes of nature, but I'd never really understood the sudden changes of people.

Pulling into our next horse motel near the Flaming Gorge in Utah, the sun was hanging low on the horizon, and we felt elated that we still had plenty of daylight left to get settled since the drive had gone according to plan. It was our first time ever to this destination, and I had made the reservation via back and forth email with the owner. A random hodgepodge of kitsch paraphernalia decorated some cabins and a tipi on a manicured patch, seemingly out of place here in the desert. There was a couple sitting outside on the deck of one of these small cabins watching us. It was unclear where we were supposed to pull the trailer in to unload the horses, so we stopped half-way into the first driveway to talk to them, happy to meet some new humans.

They weren't very happy to meet us, however. I think there might have been a sign indicating that we shouldn't park there that they pointed out, but being first-timers with a lot of stuff in the truck that we would need to haul into the cabin, I was sort of hoping we could bend the rules while we figured it out. Boy, was I wrong about that idea!

The man and woman sprang off the deck like dogs to a bone, waving their arms and explaining that heavy trailers would damage the drive. Then, when Chadeaux jumped out of the truck after many hours on the road, they made a comment about our dog not being welcome. I thought they meant she needed to be on a leash, but they said that she *wasn't welcome on property at all* and that they would need to check with their boss about this, then pointed to a "NO DOGS" sign along with all the other signs all over the building.

We'd been on the road for 6 hours. If we were not welcome here, our next planned stop was another 5 hours away. A dirt plume showed up on the hill and began following the trail down to us. When the boss arrived in a four-wheeler, I was in no mood for small talk. If we had to keep going, time was of the essence.

Her mouth was moving before she cut the engine, her opening line being, "It says on our website that no dogs are allowed in the cabins." Her demeanor was intimidating and unattractive here, and I took a step back as she moved too close for comfort into my space.

"I'm sorry – I missed that," I grimaced, exasperated. "Moreover, Chadeaux is an emotional support dog. I have the paperwork for that if that would help. If not, you are about to see me get really emotional, because I emailed you that we would be traveling with a dog over a month ago with my inquiry, and had I known she wasn't welcome, there is just no way that we ever would have agreed to come all this way. Obviously, there has been a misunderstanding, and I'm not sure what we can do to make it right, but if we need to hit the road, the sooner the better."

"No, that's true," she said wryly, as though she received pleasure out of the tough spot she had me in. "Nobody wants you to have to continue down the road at this time, we just don't want your dog in the cabin or off her leash either. She can sleep in your trailer."

"That's not going to work. She stays with us – there is no space for her to sleep in the trailer with all of our supplies. We can lay down blankets for her in the cabin. We brought all of our own bedding for the extra bed anyway."

Eventually, we came to an agreement that included an additional $50 for Chadeaux to sleep in the cabin with us. It seemed a little high on top of everything else, but we agreed that she could upcharge my account so that we would all be satisfied.

After they left, and we got the horses situated, we decided to do something to lift our spirits. Pulling out the new kid's saddle we had gotten for Tiki, I smiled as I watched Grace from the bed of the truck. She was really getting the hang of the whole "travel with horses" thing and ran around the pasture throwing hay and petting the horses in her diaper. It was adorable. Grace rode Tiki up and down the road, as I led her, and the huge smile on her face was priceless.

This beautiful moment did not change the discomfort with our hosts, and the social distance between Ruthie and I from a fight we'd had that morning. Ruthie had borrowed my friend's car to go all over Yellowstone the day before, then cut communication with us (because her phone died), and none of us knew if she was coming back until after midnight. I feared that she might have just left – she might be a goner, if you will, on the whole mission. This put my reputation on the line, since it was my employee who had disappeared with my friend's vehicle, and activated my fear that I had been left alone. As the children slept in the vehicle this morning, I chastised Ruthie, who had been working like a saint all this time. It was not my best moment, and I was still trying to make up for it, but the tension was still there.

After Grace's ride, Jenny and Jimbo, the couple that had yelled at us upon arrival, also tried to make up for everything by taking Ruthie and the girls on a tour of the chickens and donkeys. This was good for them, but I was still stuck shoveling manure out of the trailer and processing my feelings as I did. I was grateful we did not have to move on, yet I did not trust the situation and felt like a fish out of water. I recognized how often I felt like an imposter in general by not having a high-paying job of my own or fully embracing being a homemaker.

It wasn't a comfortable night. The cabin was really neat, but it was also super hot, filled with that dry desert heat that burns you from the inside out. We set up the futon on the floor for Grace and Chadeaux, while Dani and I slept in the bed. Every time the air conditioning turned on to bring the heat back down, it woke someone up. It was Ruthie's turn in the trailer, and she had the best sleep of all; in fact, she slept so well that in the morning, I thought she was gone again and had to once more work through my own fears about my part in this.

WRITE, RECORD and SHARE

Use the space below to write a few sentences, or pull out your phone and record a short video. Share it with us on social media or through my website!

When leaving a happy place, how often are you disappointed with whatever comes next?

_____

When faced with an uncomfortable accommodation or disagreeable host, how do I make the most of it?

_____

Does "making the most of it" always "work"?

_____

In challenging situations, do I find myself resenting the mundane aspects of my life even more?

_____

Do I have a big fear of being abandoned?

_____

When we are overly dependent on people, we lose sight of the great mystery all around us. As we work through disagreements and disputes, we often touch upon it. Now go, and take that first big step towards healing – you know what it is you need to do, let's do it!

Horse Motel

July 16th

In the Desert

NOT OUR PEOPLE

"He who cannot dance puts the blame on the floor."

– Hindu Proverb

The girls and I woke up around 7 am with the heat already unbearable. I began cobbling together a breakfast of oatmeal and cold Frappuccinos in those square glass bottles. Ruthie was supposed to meet me at 9 am to pack and leave by 10. Around 8 am, as I was changing Dani's diaper, she peed all over my hand. I had one diaper under the other, but neither of them was able to absorb all the urine, which cascaded onto the mattress. It was gross, and I stripped the sheets immediately and discovered there was no mattress pad on the bed, to my horror. I'd need to let this difficult staff know about that, too. Things seemed to be going from bad to worse.

The girls were getting restless, and so was I, but I couldn't shuttle them and all of our things back and forth to the trailer alone as it was parked about a quarter mile down the road now – it was just too much stuff. I started loading up the stroller and packing the cooler, knowing Ruthie would show up any minute to help me. It's always in those last minutes of transition that things get really crazy, and today was no exception as Grace threw her toothbrush in the toilet and pooped in her underwear, seemingly all at once!

Where the heck was Ruthie?? Ever since she nearly spent the night out with my friend's car, and we had a fight about it, I kept worrying that she might have left. It was 10 minutes past 9 am, and to be late was so not like her. I tried calling her cell phone, but it went straight to voicemail. From our cabin, I couldn't see if the trailer was still there, but at least it looked like our horses were. I was really ready to get out of here – NOW.

At 9:30, I dragged the infant and toddler across the desert cabin campus and knocked loudly on the trailer door to wake poor Ruthie from a deep slumber. It was so hot, I couldn't believe she was still able to sleep in a metal box. Ruthie was in good spirits about the whole thing and apologized, recognizing that her phone didn't have reception here, not that it was off, then jumped right in to help out.

As I got the horses set up with hay bags in the trailer, she took care of walking Chadeaux around the grounds with the girls, taking pictures and admiring all the weird kitschy stuff they had everywhere. If we hadn't had such a terrible reception, we might even recommend this place. That's when I saw the boss ambling towards me from the cabin that we had finally cleared out of just a few minutes before. I could tell by her walk that we were in trouble again. Thank God I had just finished loading the horses up and we were almost out of here.

"This is the part of my job I hate the most," she said, standing on her outpost deck beside the 1960s soda machine we had just gotten drinks from. "But I'm going to have to charge you another $10 for the dog hair on the futon. I have your credit card, so I'll go ahead and do that."

"How about if I just pay for that in cash? Then could we be done here?" I asked, irritated.

Her employee, Jenny, had used the same line: *this is the part of my job I hate the most,* when she came into our cabin the night before while I was breastfeeding to have me sign a receipt for being charged for the room and the horses. I had written "sent email" by the part about no dogs and signed my name to have the card charged for $175. Jenny reeked of cigarette smoke, and I thought about pointing to the chintzy sign on the wall where it said "No Pets; No smoking; Check out at 10 am." Should I have told her she'd have to bill me outside of the cabin stinking like that??

"Yeah, cash is king," she said, following me to my trailer.

I was walking with Grace on my hip. She was asking for a drink of my Cherry Cola in her cute toddler voice, and I gave it to her as we walked.

"It's all going to go straight to my staff," she said, trailing along beside me now, as Ruthie took Grace. "They're the ones who will have to pick all that hair off by hand."

Internally, I cocked my head, wondering what was going on with her managerial skills and the details of her operation. She seemed pretty out of touch with the wet details of how we had left the bed, nevermind the dry hair on the couch. Earlier, I'd let Jenny know that we had had a "pee pee accident" on the sheets in our room when I was changing Dani, and that if she got it in the wash right away, she wouldn't have to treat it.

"Did it go through the sheet?" Jenny had asked.

"Well, yes, of course it did – into the mattress comforter, so you'll have to clean that, too. I left you a note with it pulled back so you could see," and a $5 tip, I thought. I probably would have tipped $5 without the additional work, I realized. Maybe I should have left a little more, but I was just so done with this place and their strange welcome and nickel and diming attitude.

"That cover is just like a pillowcase, so it probably went all the way through to the mattress," Jenny had said lamely. I'm not sure how I responded to this, other than being apologetic and saying something offhanded about how babies, mine especially, always like to pee when you're in the middle of things — this morning I was in the middle of taking care of a poop that was so messy and major that I decided to just throw the onesie away instead of dealing with cleaning it as we traveled down the road.... I didn't tell her all that, but I later wondered what on earth was involved in cleaning those sheets, and not having a good mattress cover on there.

"I mean, people BLEED!!" I told Ruthie as we were driving down the road half an hour later. "Urine is the least of their problems. It's a hotel bed — what on earth are they thinking not having a proper mattress cover on there?! That is ridiculous."

Still, all these ideas came to me out of order later on as we traveled along, leaving me with no punchline as I stood before this boss and faced her mismanagement head on. In a way, I felt sort of sorry for her, and a bit curious about who she was and how she was making a life for herself in this desolate place. I'd seen her big fancy house on the hill overlooking all of us when I turned the trailer around by her chaparral entrance. We were clearly very different, she thriving in this landscape, me feeling parched and drained by it... craving water and movement to pass through the desert, but never to stay.

As we approached the truck, I stopped in my tracks. There, in the grill of my Red Ram, just to the right of the M on the RAM lettering, was the bird I'd hit the day before. I had heard it make contact, seen the swallow swoop from the left down towards the right, a bad judgment call on his part, with no time for us to change the course of our heavy load to avoid him.

"I hit a bird," I had told Ruthie when she looked up from the book she was reading to Grace in the back seat.

"Ohhhhh, I've done that, too," she said reassuringly. But seeing this gruesome visual the next day was disheartening.

This bird was splayed out with its white, tufted belly exposed and feces attached to the middle of it above tiny curled-up talons, like dead spiders, wings spread into different slats of the front grill of the truck, and its head... well, its head was pressed through the grill like it thought it might be a window it could pass through. Without skipping a beat, this boss lady walked right up to it and began pulling it out of my grill for me. The head was stuck, and she had to really manhandle the poor little thing, wrestling with her bare hands until it broke free. Clearly, there had been no pain as its neck must have broken upon impact. I watched, wordlessly, as she worked deftly, likely a hunter herself to be so comfortable with a dead animal. I felt squeamish and quickly gave her the $10 and thanked her for her help, shaking her hand, then regretting it as I thought about the dead bird she had just been touching.

In the truck, I put some hand sanitizer on my hands before eating but still felt unclean from the whole experience. As Ruthie and I talked a bit about it, I remembered the story of the two monks traveling in silence and celibacy. They came upon a pregnant woman struggling to cross a swollen, fast flowing river, and one of the monks picked her up and carried her across, setting her down on the other side without a word, despite it being part of their fast that they not touch or speak to women in this walk. Several hours later, the other monk was so perplexed by his partner's behavior that he finally broke his silent fast, exclaiming, "Brother, how could you pick that woman up and carry her across the river like that?! You know we are not supposed to touch women!"

"Yes," replied the older monk, "but my brother, I put her down on the other side, and here we are hours later, and you are still carrying her, aren't you?"

I wanted to put this story of the strange lady and my grumpy attitude to rest as quickly as possible. Ruthie tried to change the subject, following my lead when I said as much.

"It looks like we are going to make great time today," Ruthie said, pointing to the navigation bar on the car which said 3:21 pm arrival.

"Yeah, I'm guessing we will make it to Soft Spot Stables to drop the horses around 6," I said, calculating stops into the ETA. Then we fell silent, admiring the scenery as I focused on the drive.

This place really was gorgeous, and it distracted me from my thoughts. For the right people, I could see how this flaming gorge could be enough. For me, it only added to my unease. The thought I couldn't shake was that I just hated leaving a place feeling like, "If something went wrong, I couldn't call them." I had no idea just how much I'd wish I could do that very thing within the next hour.

WRITE, RECORD and SHARE

Use the space below to write a few sentences, or pull out your phone and record a short video. Share it with us on social media or through my website!

When I am operating from fear, how does my body physically respond?

_____

What big issue am I still carrying from the past?

_____

How will I let this go to be free for what is next?

_____

When I feel I am being taken advantage of, how do I respond?

_____

How do I address my own "roadkill"?

_____

After a difficult interaction, what do I do to prepare my mind for the next thing in my path?

_____

This is where "the rubber meets the road," as they say, and the place where a lot of the fluff of our times falls short. Reality is a big teacher. We both know it — now let's see what happens when we lose the fluff and work with it!

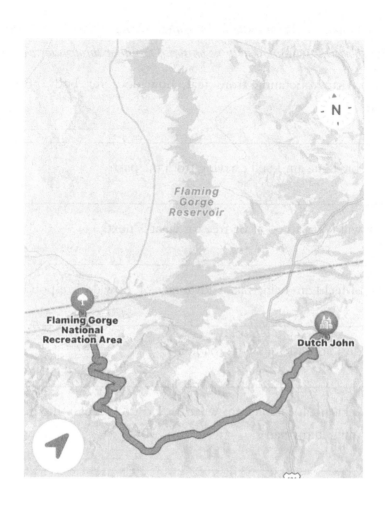

Mile 3399

July 17th

Dutch John, Utah

THE SERIAL KILLER

"We're fools whether we dance or not, so we might as well dance."

– Japanese Proverb

There was a lot of construction going on with brand new blacktop being laid on the road, and lots of angry campers and boaters zooming through it to get as much out of their vacation days as possible. I was enjoying the drive. Every mile was one step closer to our next adventure and a little more space from the weird energy of our last experience.

I'd just come up over a hill, focusing on staying in my lane, which had fresh blacktop and no paint to divide us from the traffic coming the other way, when I heard a loud pop. I looked in my left rearview mirror and saw the black tail of our tire swinging menacingly like a cat's when it is warning you it is about to scratch.

"We blew a tire," I said, putting my blinker on and slowing down in a straight line as we crested the hill.

I pulled out my phone and began dialing USRider before I even looked at it, knowing the sooner I got the call in, the sooner help would be on the way. As I punched buttons to get through to someone, confirming that my passengers and horses were safe, and allowing them to detect my exact location using radar, I unbuckled my seatbelt, opened the door, and walked back to assess the damage.

It was a good-looking flat! Wires sprung out of the tire like a poorly put together bird's nest, and stripes of tire coiled all over the ground, like those charcoal snake fireworks I loved as a kid, frozen in adult time, before they disappeared into dust, running their course. I looked down the road and saw one of our hubcaps a few hundred feet back. Ruthie was taking pictures, and I motioned for her to go get it before someone hit it as I spoke to the operator while getting back in the car to give him our exact location.

"We are about 30 miles shy of Vernal, Utah," I said, pulling up my vehicle's navigation bar.

"Did you already exit highway 44?" the operator asked. "This would help us narrow it down even more."

"Yes, we turned onto 191 and have been in a construction zone. In fact, we are still in the middle of it right now." I looked back in my sideview mirror at the large bright orange diamond shaped sign saying "ROAD WORKERS AHEAD." Might have to move that a little further down to make it easier for vehicles to get around us, I thought, also eyeing the two orange cones I'd already put up for situations like these, and confirming that my hazards were still blinking on the back of the trailer.

"I'll look around and see how fast I can get somebody there, but you guys should work on making yourselves comfortable. This is a pretty remote location, and it may take a while. An automated text will come through once we have someone on the way to change that flat."

I thanked the operator and looked at my phone: the battery was in the red. I decided to leave it in the car to charge after I texted George to let him know what was going on. I wasn't sure exactly what time it was in India, but I trusted he would get the message whenever he was supposed to. Then I got out to scout for a place to unload the horses and tie them up so they would not overheat in the trailer.

Thirty feet from where we stopped was a flat area with some stumps for sitting on and decent footing for the horses to get tied up and stand in the pines. Ruthie and I began pulling out chairs and taking turns shuttling Grace, baby Dani, horses, and water bottles back and forth. Once everyone was all set, I went back to the truck to get a water block and a bucket for the horses. I saw Grace's toy horse and some hoof cream and tossed that in the bucket, thinking I could grab a comb to get some of those nasty weeds out of Tiki's mane while we waited, giving us a few things to do.

People had been zooming by us so fast that I had put on my construction vest – I even put it on Chadeaux for a minute, knowing she would stay close to Grace and provide more visibility for our group, but it had not fit her body well, and I eventually just put it on myself once they had all climbed off the road to safety in the pines. I'd thought, sadly, *We're not in Teton Valley anymore,* remembering how two guys had jumped out of their truck with a shovel to help us pick up an unsecured bale of hay that had exploded off the back of my truck the weekend before. Regardless of where we were, my heart was still looking in the rearview.

When we first moved to Chicago, we'd been driving to a family event when we saw an Asian guy, clearly distraught, wandering along the side of the road with his hands up, a few hundred feet away from a car that was pulled over. George and I pulled over to help him, discovered that he was bloody drunk, and agreed to drive him to a gas station where his family could come get him. It became clear that this would not be his first offense if he got caught, and we knew that he was a danger to himself and others, though likely harmless on his own. We turned him over to the gas station owner to keep an eye on him, gave him the keys, and went on our way, already late, to a family function. My aunt was amazed. "I can't believe you did that!" she said. "I would NEVER do that! I mean, what if he was a serial killer or something?!"

To me, it was clear that he was just a human in a bad way in need of help – hands up in the air being the classic and most genuine international signal. As the country song goes, "I believe most people are good…" But it made me sad to hear her say this, as I wanted to believe so badly that she would slow down and help someone in need. I attributed this to the busyness of the city, where a person is just a number that you pass on your way to where you are going. In the city, few people really look at a person asking for help, or consider what they are asking for, which saddened me deeply. I prayed that I would never become so cold, fearful, or busy to stop and help someone when I could clearly see they needed it. God does not put anyone in our path by mistake.

Of course, we all have our days, and God is in charge in the end, and I'd just gotten a text in the midst of gathering buckets and water from the electronic dispatch saying that help would be on the way within 120 minutes. I called the link right away to Adam's towing, and the guy who picked up said he might be there within an hour, hour and a half, but that we should make ourselves comfortable as he was on another call right then. To cover all my bases, I let him know that we were a group with small children, that it was pretty warm, and that I had half a tank of gas to continue alternating between the AC and the heat until he got there, but the sooner the better. Then another text came in from George saying he was praying for us, and I stepped around the vehicle to see this mirage of a man walking up towards me, seemingly out of nowhere.

WRITE, RECORD and SHARE

Use the space below to write a few sentences, or pull out your phone and record a short video. Share it with us on social media or through my website!

Do you believe in miracles?

_____

When have you ever stopped for someone on the side of the road who needed help?

_____

When would you not stop?

_____

Are you more suspicious of people or more likely to believe in their innate goodness?

_____

Do you trust the process when things don't go your way?

_____

Sometimes it is when everything seems to be going wrong that the real magic is about to happen. I would love to hear (or see) your stories about this! Meanwhile, wait until you read what happens next in this one...

Mile 3594

July 17th

Vernal, Utah

THE ANGEL GABRIEL

"Dance first. Think later. It's the natural order."

— Samuel Beckett

"How you doing?" the man called out to me as we approached from 30 yards apart.

"Oh, you know… I've been better!" I chirped, wryly. "Are you with Adam's Towing? Man, you got here fast!"

"They sent Adam's?! Sheesh. You don't want those guys," he said, putting his hand out. "I'm Gabe, and I'm with a different towing company — but I just passed you, could tell you were in trouble, and thought I'd come back to see if I could help you out. You know there is a pull out just a little bit further down the road. This is a terrible spot. Let's get you down there and take care of this: what have you got — a flat?"

"That's for sure! We've got a flat, three horses, two babies, a dog, and another girl in tow," I said, motioning up to my posse in the woods fifteen feet away from the rig.

"I can see you've got your hands full!" Then he laughed to himself as we walked around to the back of the trailer where the flat was.

"Adams said they'd be here within two hours, but if you can help us out now, I'd be happy to pay you directly and cancel that call," I said, following him.

"Oh, you don't have to pay me," he said, his Utah country boy drawl shining through as he spoke. "There was a lady I wasn't

149

able to set things right with last week who gave me a terrible review. This is my opportunity to set that right by helping you out when I'm the first to come across you."

"We can definitely do that! Oh my God, I'd be so grateful – we still have another four hours of driving to go to get to our destination tonight in Colorado. I'll do whatever I can to write up a good review for you and your company," I promised.

"That would be great," he said. Then, all business, he continued, "But first thing's first – let's get you and your family to that pull-out down the road for safety. I really don't like this spot with everyone speeding by like idiots because of the construction."

"How shall we do that?" I asked, gesturing to my group.

"You drive, and I can help move these horses if you want – it's really not far."

"Do you know anything about horses?" I knew this was a rhetorical question by the look of his jeans, boots, and belt buckle, and I was hardly able to believe my luck as God put this person together, this diamond in the flaming gorge rough to help us here and now – it was totally surreal.

"Born and raised on a ranch, and we've got horses and cows, and I'm totally comfortable around your horses," he replied, coolly, not that anything needed to be said with the way he was dressed.

"Wow. I can't believe this!" I said, not knowing what else to say. Then we devised a plan, with him walking the two mares, including the palomino, who could be a little oblivious about personal space. Ruthie walked Jet with the baby strapped on her front side, while I drove Grace and Chadeaux in the car another eighth of a mile down the road where, sure enough, there was a pull out.

When they caught up to me, I lamented, "Well, this was a real lesson to just walk down the road a bit and see if there isn't a better spot just around the bend. I wasn't sure what was next – it could have been a big drop off."

"Well, actually, there is a huge mountain pass coming where a lot of people blow out their brakes. It's the truckers who always test it, and I get to see what it looks like when they flunk and it goes wrong. Are you comfortable using your compression brake system?"

"Uhhhh… you mean my Jake brake?" I asked. This was a function I did not have on my first diesel truck, which was nearly 20 years older, but I loved using it on my 2018 "Red Beauty," that I had purchased for this road trip. She was pulling through all this stuff like a dream.

"Yeah – that's the one," he said as we got familiar with the location of my jack in the new vehicle under the front passenger's seat. While we did this, he looked up at a white truck driving by with another trailer on it and said, "I can't believe it," not knowing what else to say. "That was my best friend who just drove by, and he didn't even stop! I'm going to have to call him on that."

I smiled and graciously reminded him, "With all due respect, sir, most people don't stop." Then I changed the subject. "Do you know I actually had to call the dealer to try to find the tire change kit – in the manual, it just says something about taking out your kit to change a flat but nothing about where to find it!"

"Most of them are here now, but all of them are a little

different," he explained.

"My last truck was so old, it didn't have a place for all that stuff, so I knew exactly where it was – in the trunk on top of my auxiliary tank." I took a breath to reflect on this.

He began dissecting the kit and showing me what all the parts were for, including things I probably never would have thought of. "See this?" He held up a circular pyramid. "This is a funnel for if you have to get gas into your tank remotely. They're pretty complete now – they have thought of everything."

I was grateful to know where all of this was and to witness his work. He used a combination of my jack kit and his own tools to lift the wheel and change the tire. It was fascinating to pick up some tricks of the trade from a pro, like how he let the wheel spin with the crank to minimize his effort and maximize the turning production to pull the bolts off. Then he looked at the tread on the other tire and whistled: it had to go. Even I could see that.

"It didn't look like that when we got to Teton Valley – I swear to God. Then again, the last time I really checked it was in Montana, when we had all that trouble with a hot axle and had to change a tire off the other side… what do you think would cause that tread to wear like that?"

"Ohhhh…. I've got some ideas, but I don't want to tell you what they are because it might scare the be-Jesus out of you." He was still laying down under the trailer, wrestling with the snake strands of tire that had wrapped themselves very tightly around the axle joint because we drove it to this pull out.

"Sheesh," I shuddered and swallowed. Seeing he was tied up for a while, I went to tell Ruthie what he had said and nurse baby Dani, who was up in the shade with the horses. We both raised our eyebrows. Nursing brought my heart rate down again and made me feel okay.

"Did you see his name?" she asked, giving me a knowing look, as she helped Grace with getting some peanut butter on her celery.

"What do you mean?" I hadn't really thought about it.

"Gabe," she said, then waited for me to fill in the punchline as she looked up between sprinkling raisins on the "log." I stared at her blankly, wondering what Biblical passage or sermon I must have slept through. Was it Cain and Gabel?

"The ANGEL Gabriel!" she finally stammered, incredulous that I had missed this sign. I'm not so good with my angels, but I was pretty sure that Gabriel had something to do with telling Mary she would have Jesus and that he was an Archangel. I later looked all this up when I was having trouble sleeping that night and learned that in the old testament he is considered an archangel, but that in the new testament, he is "just an angel." This is when I begin to drift from religious details: I mean, isn't an angel an angel? In this scenario, he clearly was one with skin on.

"Oh wow, I hadn't thought of that! That is so cool. Good thinking, Ruthie." I gave her a high five, then gave her baby Dani as "the angel Gabriel" returned to us.

"You're all set," he said matter of factly.

"God bless you, sir," I replied, smiling as Grace climbed on my hip. "Besides a review, is there anything more we can do for you? You've been so good to us, getting us on the road so quickly and generously. Can I give you a beverage? We have tea and some bubbly drinks…"

"I'll take anything carbonated," he said happily, gratefully accepting the cold LaCroix I pulled out of the cooler. "And I know what you can do for me – you can take me riding on one of your horses." I sized him up. It was hard to tell his age. He could have been anywhere from 24 to 44… maybe 40. Was he hitting on me? His request seemed innocent enough.

"Oh, Gabe, I would love nothing more than to take you riding, but it's not going to be today, because we really need to get down the road. Tell you what, next time we pass through, we will for sure take you out for a ride!" I promised, not knowing what else to say.

"There are lots and lots of great trails around here – I could show you a thing or two," he said, like a true local.

"That would be awesome. I would love that," I said, and I meant it. But we had miles to go before it might ever happen again, and a fire to put out now, so I persevered, asking, "Meanwhile, where should we go to fix this tire?"

"Go to Jack's – they're the best in Vernal," he said without skipping a beat.

"Is there someone in particular I should ask for?" I laughed, as he had his phone out and was already dialing and nodding as he said, "Hey, John, I've got this lady here…."

Ruthie and I went about our business of loading the girls, animals, and things back up and preparing to sit down and nurse as soon as he left. Our GPS projected 40 minutes to Jack's, where John was expecting us to put on two tires. Gabe said something about needing to drop the truck off that he was working on when he stopped for us, but that he might see us there since he had some other business to attend to in the area. I was sorry to see him go. It had been really nice to let someone else take charge of a difficult situation and just bask in receiving help and direction. The fact that he arrived within seconds of my husband praying was not lost on me, and I felt chills of gratitude.

WRITE, RECORD and SHARE

Use the space below to write a few sentences, or pull out your phone and record a short video. Share it with us on social media or through my website!

Do you believe in divine intervention?

_____

Are you open to receiving all life has to offer?

_____

Describe a miraculous meeting in your own life:

_____

How could THE plan be better than your own plan?

_____

When have locals given big insights on your journey?

_____

Have you found someone who knows how to do what it is that you need done to continue on the dream?

_____

You know what's coming, and sometimes you don't — that is why it is important to have a guide who can show you the way. If you have not found them yet, reach out! There will be other guides you cannot plan for, but it is always best to begin with a teacher to point you in the right direction.

Mile 3666

July 17th

Green Pasture in Utah

STOKING THE FLAMES OF COMFORT

"What if I want to go as hard as I can on something that
comes easily to me?"

– Marie Forleo

The tire shop had a clean, air conditioned office with some of
the friendliest office staff I've ever met. After getting the trailer
set up in a garage with shade for the horses and a jack that could
lift them safely, we retreated from the desert heat with Chadeaux,
who they welcomed with open arms. While the mechanics
changed the first tire and looked at the rest of them, which would
probably also need to go, we got cozy in the waiting area.

There were huge tires of various sizes decorating the space
which became our new "play zone." A secretary brought out
some toys and games they kept on hand for children and invited
us to use a break room with a table and chairs to eat our snacks.
The walls were decorated with more busts of elk and deer than I
could count, and I taught Grace how to count the antler tips on
each one. The owner came in and began telling us about his
various hunting escapades. They felt like "my people." It felt
good to feel welcomed, to feel at home.

The next thing I knew, Gabe was in the parking lot with a
shiny truck and gooseneck trailer. He explained that he had a
plan. While his friends changed the rest of our tires, he would
load our horses up in his trailer and drive them back to his place.

On the way, we could drop our trailer off at his business for his guys to take a look at and make sure there wasn't anything else off that was contributing to the tires wearing unevenly, so we could avoid future breakdowns. Safety was our first priority, of course.

I was stunned, and glad, to see him again. Something about this plan felt a little bit like a Mormon thing, with the "men taking care of the women and children." I did a check-in with myself to make sure I still felt okay with this arrangement and asked a few more questions. Apparently, his wife was already expecting us, and his children were looking forward to playing with our children while we waited. The horses could graze in a back pasture, and Ruthie and I were welcome to take naps there as well. Clearly, everyone's needs would be met with this amazing plan, and I realized I was more than ok with being taken care of in this way – I was eternally grateful. It was nice to let someone else be in charge.

We agreed, and everything unfolded smoothly. In fact, it was even better than I possibly could have imagined. The grass pasture was huge, and our horses took off happily to graze it. I had not seen them this happy since we left Wyoming. They had pigs, chickens, and goats to entertain the children, and his wife and kids were gracious hosts. Like the Biblical story, I felt that if they'd had a goose to slaughter, they would have run around trying to catch it for us.

Gabe hooked up our trailer and took it to his shop. Meanwhile, Ruthie and I took turns resting in our truck with the windows down, soaking up the cool Utah breeze, or hanging out with his wife and playing with his children in his living room. Our kids were in 7th heaven with these new playmates, and their Barbies and toys. There wasn't exactly an invitation to stay the night, but we were also not in a hurry to go, because all of our needs were being met so perfectly. It was easy to wait when we felt so at home.

The only thing better than this would be a home of our own, my family's home, which was our next stop. I craved a familiar bed, and we only had two more nights before George would get there. We'd lost several hours now, and if we carried on, we wouldn't get there until after midnight, but I couldn't help it. I wanted to sleep in a familiar bed. Even with all of this hospitality and a miracle of a day, when he told us our trailer was good to go, I felt the need to press on. After eating pizza together, which we happily bought, we hit the road.

Like Teton Valley, a part of me was left behind in this experience. It was so comfortable being with this other family. Gabe had had his whole team of mechanics check our trailer out and barely charged us. It was more than we deserved. Juxtaposed against the horrific reception we'd had only 24 hours before, this experience was especially miraculous. Little did I know that more miracles were waiting for us down the road.

WRITE, RECORD and SHARE

Use the space below to write a few sentences, or pull out your phone and record a short video. Share it with us on social media or through my website!

Name the biggest thing you have ever let go of:

_____

What would having all the needs of your dependents and coworkers met look like?

_____

How do I define gender roles in my marriage and my life?

_____

Am I able and willing to pay for what I need?

_____

Am I living beyond my physical and spiritual capacity?

_____

What would being aligned in all the big areas of my life look like?

_____

If you could have a do-over on your upbringing, what might you do differently?

_____

Congratulations on GOING BIG in Part 2! How we are born and raised can feel really big – it is one of the few things we can escape. Sure, we may change things, but there are some aspects of ourselves and our beliefs that will stay with us, regardless of what we do on the outside. This is why it is important to know how and when to go home, and have a true understanding of what home means… let's go there!

Part 3:

How to Go Home

At the end of the day, no matter how heavy our load, or how long our road is, we all come home. Sometimes home does not feel like the hallmark themes our culture feeds us; it may feel disjointed, automatic, temporary, disrupted, or even disturbed. What if we have to get uncomfortable in order to get comfortable? What if the ultimate comforts of home that we seek have been inside us all along?

Invitation: If you want to see images of the journey home, and the creature comforts we accessed along the way, please mosey on over to my website and check out my free workshop that includes pictures and a process to find your own way home.

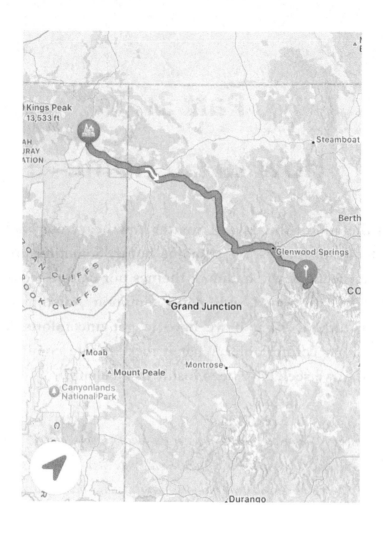

Mile 3895

July 17th

Snowmass, CO

JESUS WAS THERE

"I don't want people who want to dance, I want people who have to dance."

– George Balanchine

Lots of people asked if I lost weight on the trip. Ironically, I didn't lose a single pound, but I didn't gain any weight either. What people were noticing was that my body and confidence, my outlook, completely changed upon my return, although the number on the scale hadn't moved. In the weight loss world, we call these "NSVs" or non-scale victories, and managing to take the trip at all was a victory, just like managing to maintain my sanity through an unexpected quarantine for a month or more is a win. Instead of focusing on gaining or losing, now I'm focused on showing up and being the best person I can be in each moment, just like I did on the trip. It's not about the weight, by the way – it never is. Knowing this at your core is big, far bigger than your "goal weight!"

A huge motivator in continuing the journey that day was not just a comfortable bed, but a home in which I could engage in some long overdue self-care things, like shaving my legs and taking a bubble bath with the girls. The "things" we were doing had more to do with how they made us feel, not only after, but in the process of doing them, than they did with "looking good" or "smelling good" for others, although this was an important side effect. If there was one thing I had learned about a healthy relationship with one's body and soul, it was that it had to both feel good and serve one spiritually as a positive practice. For example, a cookie may taste good and satisfy a craving for being with one's mom who always made that kind of cookie, but if we are doing that 5 times a day, 7 days a week, it's not healthy. A few cookies now and then, or even once a day in conjunction with a healthy meal plan – and a body that isn't overly sensitive to sugar – IS GOOD, because it is so for the body and the soul. It is all about moderation.

Moderation seemed to be something we had thrown out the window as we headed south and the sun began to set low in the summer sky. Ruthie was at the wheel, winding down another single lane riverbed with huge tan cliffs on our right side and a dropoff to the left where a river presumably ran far below us. Up ahead, we saw writing scrawled across the cliff face in an organized way, not quite like graffiti, though it was. It said "Jesus was here." Ruthie started pulling her phone out to take a picture of it as she rounded the turn, veering into the oncoming lane as she did. Then she corrected, as I barked something about Jesus not wanting us to get in an accident to know he was here. OR maybe it said, "Jesus is coming." Either way, we could feel God all around us in our circumstances, just like we had when the kayak was in the middle of the road as we entered the big country of Idaho. We were lucky to be here, to be alive, and to be steering around the hazards, and seeing the signs that we saw.

A few miles later, we pulled over to get gas, snacks, and change the girls into their pajamas as the sun was setting. I knew this last two-hour stretch of road quite well, and I also knew that cops and deer roamed frequently over these hills, so I wanted to be the one behind the wheel. I'd been pulled over more than once for speeding here, which always reminded me of how I had grown up "in a hurry to get things done," as the country song goes, "I rush and rush until life's no fun." If there was one thing that this trip and working with horses and children had taught me, it was that we all need to slow down. "Nature does not hurry, yet everything is accomplished," said Lao Tzu, and I contemplated this as I chased the sun down into darkness.

The truck was silent, except for the music playing low to keep me awake as the adrenaline wore off. I could hear a delicate toddler snore coming from the backseat. I had to pull off for coffee a few times and had a bit of an issue getting on the freeway as a result of some construction, poor signage, and weird loop-de-loops, but now we were on course to arrive around 10 or 10:30 pm at Soft Spot Ranch. I was excited about keeping our horses there because I used to go there for summer camps as a kid. Despite the horses having to be quarantined away from everyone, the benefits of being able to stay at a place from my childhood outweighed the cons. Moreover, I hadn't been able to find anything closer to my family's home anyway.

I'd been in communication with the barn manager over the past few months with increasing frequency as we got closer to the arrival date. Colorado, and the West as a whole, had been struggling with terrible forest fires, which was not uncommon this time of year. What was different was that they were happening in the very valley where we were headed – it was literally "close to home." Needless to say, we'd been in correspondence regarding evacuation procedures and just how close the fires were to the ranch itself. On the day of travel, the fires were only about 20 miles down the valley, which was close enough to feel the burn and have some side effects, but I had no idea what they would be until much later.

Driving a familiar stretch of road that became even more familiar as we neared our destination had a meditative effect on me. I was in a trance-like state, anticipating each sign, stoplight, and curve when I saw it. Up on the ridge in front of me was a blaze of fire. The whole hillside was red. It was a fierce and breathtaking reminder that nature was in control of this valley, not us.

At the next red light in Basalt, I took a picture of the smoke and fire, literally only 100 yards or so away above us. It was a humbling reminder of the hell this community and many others had gone through in the past few years. Friends of ours in Southern California had literally had their homes explode when the wildfire ran through it, and they'd lost everything. The images were akin to a war zone – a war with nature.

As the light turned green, I said prayers for all those suffering and our four-legged family, who would be on the "front lines" if the fire continued moving as it had been. When we pulled into Soft Spot, it was closer to 11 pm, and no one was around. I had trouble finding the quarantine pens in the dark, as well as the lay of the land since we planned to leave our trailer there instead of trying to take it into my family's residential neighborhood.

After getting the horses set up with water and feed in their individual pens, I scouted the area on foot with the light of my cell phone and the hazel glow of moonlight through the smoke. It appeared that everyone had their trailers stored on top of this hill adjoining their pens. There was a steep access road to get to it, but the footing seemed good, and our trailer was in a perfect position to do it, especially without the weight of the horses in there. I floored it, hooting under my breath as I did. This was my favorite kind of backcountry driving, and I was excited to have an opportunity to use my new truck on a steep grade.

We bounced over the hill and managed to unhook the trailer in the dark and load a few personal items and duffels into the bed of the truck before heading down the road. The caretaker of my family's home had already turned the alarm off, and the code for the garage was the same as it had been almost 30 years before when it was first built. Ruthie had been there with us a few months before for a spring break ski trip, so we set to work getting Grace's room set up and settling into our own rooms without much conversation. We were tired.

Waking up in the master bedroom with Dani the next day was one of the happiest moments of my life. Finally, we had arrived in a place where we could all fit. We were safe. We were alive. It was so humbling. I could feel that everyone's needs were truly being met, that, once again, we'd "done it." Moreover, in some ways, we were home, here in the mountains, in a home I had been coming to since I was a child. I felt grateful for my grandparents' hard work in building this home, and all my relations in maintaining it.

The only thing that was missing were the horses, because there was no space for them at my family's vacation home. Eight miles felt really far away given everything we had been through in the last few days, and they were that many miles closer to the active forest fire. The stress of that fire near them juxtaposed against the high level of comfort we humans were experiencing with Chadeaux made me feel guilty, and I turned to prayer for peace.

WRITE, RECORD and SHARE

Use the space below to write a few sentences, or pull out your phone and record a short video. Share it with us on social media or through my website!

Do you have a home for mixed feelings?

_____

When your animals are placed in a less than ideal home, how does that make you feel?

_____

Define the standards you have for a home of your own:

_____

Would you drive through a fire to "sleep in your own bed?"

_____

After a life-threatening experience, what would you pay to go home?

_____

Hooray – you have started the process of bringing it all home! Our homes are a reflection of all that we are hauling and what seems big to us. They are not just the physical spaces we live in, they are also our bodies and minds, our spiritual homes. Let's continue!

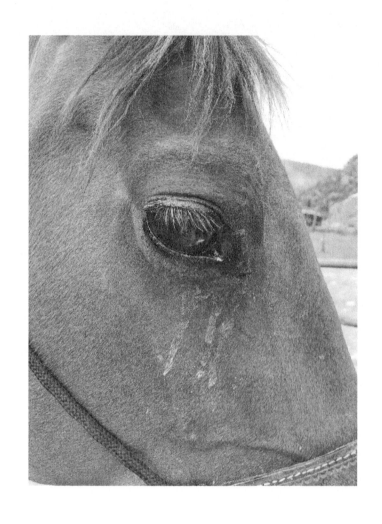

Mile 3925

July 18th

Pitkin County, CO

MIDNIGHT LOVER

"The body says what words cannot."

– Martha Graham

After a lazy breakfast in my family's home, I headed 8 miles down the road to check on the herd with Grace while Ruthie and baby Dani chilled out with Chadeaux. Living with horses, we fostered a relaxed rhythm, which included being adaptable to changes in environment, feed, spacing, and structure. I had been giving the horses a probiotic supplement to help them manage the many stressors, especially when it came to what was put in their tummies or how much exercise they got. The girls sometimes participated in holding a hose to fill buckets of water or scoop feed, but more often than not, they observed or played in the space while Ruthie and I got things done.

Soft Spot Stables was made for family fun, and we enjoyed exploring and meeting the summer campers and miniature ponies. Grace was a good helper leading the horses to turn them out in the sand arena and letting them run and roll outside of their 15-by 20-foot independent quarantine pens, which were hundreds of feet away from any other horses. While they played in the arena, we explored the gift shop and bought snacks and a tiny purple helmet that fit Grace perfectly and made her smile.

I was satisfied that the horses were in good shape, except Solita, who had puss streaming out of her eyes. This was likely due to the smoke from the nearby forest fire, and I dug into my vet kit to find the eye ointment my vet had sold me preemptively to manage any sort of eye issues like this. Then I put fly masks on them, which are sort of like sunglasses, to manage the glare, since their pens had no shade.

While I managed all of this and prepped feed for the next day so that we could take a day off from coming to the farm, a man came up to us and began asking me questions about my truck. I'd seen him eyeing us from a distance for a few hours and was relieved when he finally came up and introduced himself and his intentions. I showed him the Ram Boxes and the tailgate extender, along with the extra space for storage behind the cab seat. He was impressed and asked how it compared to other brands on the market. I'd traded out my 17-year-old diesel Chevy Silverado for this 2018 Ram 2500 Cummings diesel and told him we couldn't be happier. It was fun to share in the joy of trucks and farm life. He told us a bit about working at Soft Spot and some of the hay and fire situations they'd been dealing with. I was reminded that horses bring a community together and that it takes a village.

As we drove away, I couldn't help but feel socially distant from our horses. This was the farthest we had been from them since the trip started, and it felt like I was literally leaving them out by a smoking campfire while we stayed in a castle 8 miles away on a hill, with relatively clean indoor air to breathe. Still, we needed a break, and I had done everything to prepare for a day off from caring for them, getting everything lined up with the staff there. But no one is ever going to love or care for someone's horses the way their owner will, and I was going to get a rude awakening about that in no time.

Meanwhile, George was coming in late that evening, and I had to get some groceries and a few other things situated. After we put the girls to bed, I was getting ready to go and pick him up when I saw the text about his plane being delayed. Ultimately, we agreed that he should take a cab as it looked like he wouldn't end up getting in until 1 am, since they kept pushing it back. I was excited to get reunited with my partner, but I was more excited about getting to sleep at a reasonable hour, exhausted by the trip itself and all the decisions I had made on my own.

He came in like a midnight lover out of the darkness, and we got reacquainted, which was even more romantic in its own right. In the morning, the girls squealed with delight at seeing their Daddy, hugging him and squeezing him to make sure he was really there. Ruthie took the truck into Aspen for a break of her own, and we spent the day around the house, taking a short walk to the pond with Chadeaux and the girls. All seemed right with the world, but some important members of our family were missing... and soon, they would remind us how much we had missed out by not visiting them that day.

The next day we rested again in the morning before going to the truck to go see the horses. There was a huge dent on the tailgate. It was upsetting because it was a brand-new truck and because I had no idea where it might have come from. For a minute, I became suspicious of the nice man who had spent so much time talking to me about my truck. I told George about it – was it possible he put a dent in my truck? It didn't make sense.

As we drove the 8 miles down the valley to Soft Spot and arrived on scene, we were able to put it together. That first night that I took the rig over the big hill, the trailer and truck must have kissed (badly) on a sharp angle. It made perfect sense that my problems were of my own making, and I tried to keep a sense of humor about it just being a thing, but I was annoyed with myself for having been so careless. My partner made me feel better, reminding me that everyone was safe and that what we were doing was heroic in its own right. Then we got down to business by doing "the needful" for our horses.

WRITE, RECORD and SHARE

Use the space below to write a few sentences, or pull out your phone and record a short video. Share it with us on social media or through my website!

Do you feel at home with your partner?

Is your vehicle an extension of your home?

What "things" are needed to bring you, your children, and your animals back to a place of homeostasis?

Describe how rest feels in your own home:

If home is where the heart is, then it would follow that everyone in our hearts would be in our home... but that is not how it works in our society. Take a moment to share what is on your heart about your home and all those you find in it. Feel free to reach out to me — I would love to know more!

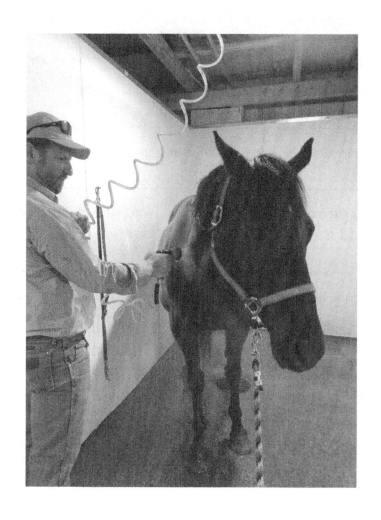

Mile 4000

July 21st

Near Wildfires

THE MISSED DAY

"In human intercourse, the tragedy begins not when there is misunderstanding about words, but when silence is not understood."

– Henry David Thoreau

They say prevention is the best medicine. For the most part, I think this is true, but there are always going to be times when things just don't go your way. In Paulo Coelho's The Alchemist, there is a story about a boy who needs to take in all the sights in a beautiful palace while carrying a spoon full of oil and not spilling a drop. The secret is to stay focused on both, but inevitably, you spill or miss something.

I had missed something. George and I went to visit the horses in the evening and prep more buckets for the following day, and as soon as we arrived, I knew we had a problem. The sun was setting, but beneath the brilliant pink glow, I could see that Jet was not feeling well.

He had his front leg up and pawed at the air uncomfortably, as though he were trying to stretch something out but couldn't quite satisfy the need. Jet's black coat had a sheen of sweat as his body struggled to produce a bowel movement. This was not the first time I had seen this; Jet was in a full-blown colic.

Horse people cringe at the sound of colic the way most cringe at the sound of COVID-19. Some of the similarities are that it can be both deadly and mild, but it's hard to tell which one you are in until it is often too late, so you need to act quickly. The first step was to get Jet walking around, trying to move it through with exercise. He really wanted to lay down and roll. People have differing opinions about this – there is a very rare situation where rolling in the middle of a colic can lead to a twisted gut, which will kill a horse immediately. As a precaution, many say not to let horses roll at all during a colic, because if that happens, you can't get them up, and it's suddenly over.

My gut said that if he needed to roll, I was going to let him trust his instincts. After all, in the wild, he would be able to do whatever he wanted, and nature would run its course. Over and over, colic reminded me that although I was responsible for doing my part to save his life, I was ultimately not in control of whether he lived or died. At the farthest reaches of this scary situation loomed the dreaded decision about whether or not to operate. Opening up a horse for colic surgery costs $5000, and then the real cost of the surgery begins, depending on what is done and how many days would follow in 24-hour vet care bills during the rehabilitation in a horse hospital. A friend of mine had elected to open her mule up, paid $8000 in full, and still had her mule die on the operating table.

Although I hoped I'd never be tested on this philosophy, I did not believe that surgery made sense. So, we began walking and gave Jet a very common medicine called "Banamine" which serves to loosen up the bowels and produce a bowel movement. Unlike people, horses cannot throw up if they eat a rock or bad food. Instead, it gets stuck in their enormous guts, and the impaction can kill them or cause the extreme signs of distress we call colic in the horse world.

Another groom at the stables who I had befriended suggested

that we hose him down with water to cool him off, as he was sweating and because he had been out all day in the sun without being able to lay down. We agreed, in part because with colic you usually try everything and the kitchen sink before calling the vet for stronger drugs and options.

I had called the barn manager and gotten the information for the local veterinarian who was on call that night. The vet was based in Glenwood Springs about 45 minutes up the valley, so we knew that whenever we called, it was safe to say there would be at least an hour of lead time. We pressed on with our various remedies and prayed. No matter what happened, I was going to blame myself for this, and I felt the weight of that.

Ruthie had ridden Jet for the first time in Montana and had switched from having the mare, Solita, be her favorite to "the dark horse." Jet was quite a looker, a real black beauty, and he loved to work and show off his muscles under saddle. When she rode him, I could tell they were now a good match energetically – she no longer feared him. I could feel the power and magic of her prayers and love when a rainbow appeared in the distance, a special symbol between Ruthie and her mother. I just prayed it wasn't going to be a sign of the transitory nature of life for Jet.

I'd had Jet since I first got sober when I was a caretaker for a woman with a herd of about five horses at the base of the mountains in Wilson, Wyoming. Jet had taught me the power of working with my fear and getting back in the saddle. The first time I rode him, he threw me off, and my friend, an old Vietnam vet horseshoer had said, "Cat, there ain't a horse that can't be rode and there ain't a cowboy that can't be throwed." I chuckled as I got back on, but my left pinky hurt. After that, it was forever bent, as I likely walked off a broken knuckle joint, as most cowgirls do. Oops.

So I'd learned to respect him from the ground and appreciate how sensitive he was. As we walked and prayed, I kept my hand on him, considering how all of this must feel in his eyes. We went from home to several different sites all along the country with huge hauls in the trailer in between them. He must have been so relieved to leave the high humidity of the midwest and return "home" to the green pastures in the cool mountain air with the old herd that he'd spent three years of his life with in Idaho before we'd had children and moved. After ten days there, we had moved to a strange, dusty desert climate. The next day, we had another breakdown with more trailer changes, then grazing and leaving another luscious green pasture, before finally arriving "home" to a smoky quarantine pen. The day after that, I had shown up to turn them out in a sand arena, give everyone eye ointment, hardly spending any time with them because I was exhausted. So then, the next day, I took a day off, and he had to process all of this without his master – he must have felt so abandoned. No wonder he had colicked.

I felt sick to my stomach just thinking about it, and I prayed for self-forgiveness and wisdom going forward throughout the rest of our trip. We were about 2/3 of the way through, but we still had a long way to go before we'd be home again… and many years before any one of us died, I hoped. No matter how Jet went to his final pasture, I felt I would blame myself and tried to keep the faith and trust God in this and all things. Only God knew for sure how this would all pan out.

WRITE, RECORD and SHARE

Use the space below to write a few sentences, or pull out your phone and record a short video. Share it with us on social media or through my website!

Do you take your responsibilities home with you?

_____

Is it possible that you are taking on more responsibility than is due you?

_____

How do you face yourself in the mirror when you feel you have failed?

_____

Is your home a safe place to recover?

_____

What recovery practices do you have in place already?

_____

When things go wrong with our homes or our animals, we can tend to blame ourselves. I heard someone say that no matter how someone dies, you will blame yourself for it. This is why it is so important to have a practice and a coach to get you out of that thinking and into a new spiritual home in your head around responsibility. Have you found yours yet? Please, reach out.

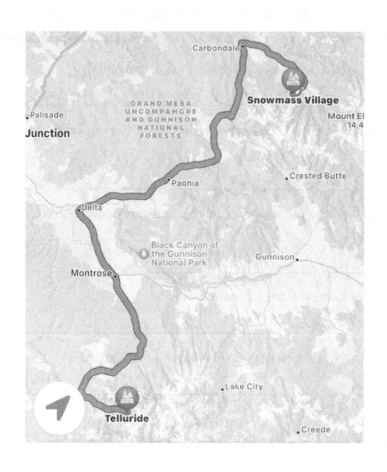

Mile 4275

July 22nd

Telluride, CO

CALL US THEN

"The truth hurts, but silence kills."

– Mark Twain

Eventually, much to everyone's relief, Jet did pull through. George was walking him around the indoor sand arena under the lights so we could watch his breathing and body more easily while I talked to the groom from the sidelines about how we thought he was doing. When his tail lifted and that little pile of horse manure peeked out, we all cheered. It was over, thank God, and Jet would live another day.

We were exhausted, but I was also concerned about how this scare had woken me up to be more hyper-vigilant and cautious about the next leg of our journey. Things had just changed – again. Originally, we had planned to keep our horses down in Ouray, even further away than they were here, about an hour from where we'd be staying. I had not been able to "crack the code" of horse people in Telluride, so had settled on Ouray for our week there. In the interim, I had made a lot of contacts, however, including an unusual group that was in the process of raising money for and building "The Telluride Horse Park."

When we'd spoken on the phone, they'd made it clear that they were too "early on" in their building and permitting process to accommodate boarders. "We don't have any water hooked up, we have to haul it all in," he told me over the phone, as one demonstration of why it wouldn't work out. "Eventually, we would love to put up horsecampers and people passing through like you, but we just aren't set up yet." I'd graciously accepted their boundary but secretly hoped something might work out.

Now it was time to call them and pray that we could make a deal. If our horses were at the horsepark in Telluride, they'd be about 10 minutes away from where we were staying in a rental condo up on the mountain for our family retreat. I also called the owner of the condo who said he had a lot across the street with his business partner and that he would be willing to let us put up our electric wire on it and keep the horses right on site. Although this sounded dreamy, and we even scouted it with Google Earth, it was not a good setup for a full week. We could manage for a night or two, but three horses would graze an acre down really quickly, and then they would likely test the electric fence and residential neighborhood in search of greener pasture. It seemed too risky.

Another idea was to have no plan and see what happened if we were fueled exclusively on faith and the belief that everything would work out perfectly. This meant we would say our prayers and head into Telluride by way of the mountain pass and knock on the doors of some unbeknownst horse person and beg to rent a pasture, given our recent colic scare. I had plenty of ideas. Surely one of them would land – and everything would work out as it should!

Luckily, the stars had aligned for my first wish to come true, and the friendly founders of the Telluride Horse Park agreed to work with us given the circumstances. We came up with a donation fee and a list of our respective duties and rules for riding around their park, then agreed to meet a few hours later in downtown Telluride so they could check us out and lead us there. This would all be under the radar as we did not want to mess with their permitting process.

On the way over, we stopped and took the horses out for a ride along a creek bed in the mountains. Ruthie put the girls in the stroller for some fresh air, knowing they would fall asleep as she walked and took photographs. Chadeaux followed as George and I rode our horses up the canyon until we found a spot to go take a swim. It was heaven.

The horses drank in the clear mountain water and soaked their legs in the cool stream before we loaded them back up, and I finally felt like I could breathe again, that the best was yet to come. We were going to meet really cool people and have an incredible week with friends and family. It had always been my dream to bring horses here, and now this dream was coming true.

As we pulled into Telluride, my breath was taken away again by the beauty of the mountains here in summer, with wildflowers and waterfalls. Then, to top it off, a giant rainbow stretched over the valley as if God was smiling upside down at us. Once again, we had arrived.

WRITE, RECORD and SHARE

Use the space below to write a few sentences, or pull out your phone and record a short video. Share it with us on social media or through my website!

How do you know when you have arrived?

_____

What feels like home to our animals?

_____

Where do home and "God's country" meet?

_____

When seeking homes along the journey, have you ever found an even better home than your original plan?

_____

If not, imagine and describe it:

_____

Home is a way of being, actually, and trusting in a bigger plan. This journey showed me that again and again! Next, we play with climbing the mountain and then coming home again: read on…

Mile 4362

July 23rd

San Miguel County, CO

THEY DON'T WANT TO FALL EITHER

"Those who were seen dancing were thought to be insane by those who could not hear the music."

– Friedrich Nietzsche

It took me a while to realize that even in doing something that my parents openly disapproved of, I was still seeking their approval. We had seen them for Dani's baptism a month before we left, and my mom had asked my friend to talk me out of it. I felt triumphant having made it this far, and disappointed that they failed to even see our horses with us. It was great to see my parents, but I found myself no longer having patience for this old dance between us. I was grateful that we were all here attending a Recovery Conference, because addictions can run in the family, and I wondered if some part of me was addicted to my parents' approval?

This was when I recognized that although I may have been in the past, I had changed. Now I found substitute parental figures who believed in our mission and lifestyle with horses, because it felt that my parents did not. Actually, I had a pattern of doing this since adolescence. *We get the parents we need, not the ones we want.* For example, I had engaged in this huge trip whether they liked it or not, and I had left home for boarding school at the age of 14 without looking back, having only lived with my parents for a few consecutive months in my teens and twenties between jobs or trips, and was ruthlessly independent with my decisions, because I had to be.

In my family, you are either running away from something or fighting for it. Few members seem to occupy a neutral ground. I tend to be a runner, but this trip was a catch-22 because I was fighting for something I believed in, running away from something I wanted to escape, and running toward it, all whilst trying to stay neutral about what was happening in the moment. My goal was to be at peace no matter what happened and find the friends or tribe who wanted to be part of that.

My father's brother, Uncle Tom, and his wife, Aunt Ranya, who were also there for the Recovery Conference, turned out to be my tribe. We took them out for a ride with the founders of the Horsepark and had a beautiful family adventure bonding together. Then we ponied Grace around in her new purple helmet and did some grooming and chores together. I could see that they were showing up for us and witnessing the profundity of what we were doing, and loving it as much as we were. I was grateful to share this experience together with my family.

Although I invited my dad to come out with us for a ride, he preferred to go fishing by himself or with other friends and only succeeded in driving by the park and seeing our horse trailer from a distance once, or so he said. Ironically, he seemed upset that I went out riding with another friend of his, named Wave, who I recognized was a bit like my substitute horse father. He had grown up on a ranch and had horses of his own, and he was game to take a ride with us, unlike my own father, despite the invitation.

Because he had more experience, we decided to head out on one of our bigger missions with him, a loop trail that the founders of the Horsepark had recommended which wasn't too far away. As we drove up the valley to the trailhead, I was blown away by the beauty of the Colorado Rockies. There were cattle grazing and old homestead properties along the way, and everything seemed right with the world. We had packed lunches, snacks, and refreshments for ourselves and the horses and were looking forward to heading out for a few hours in the wilderness.

After I got Jet's saddle on and tightened his cinch, he began bucking like a wild bronco. This was not totally out of the ordinary, but I had not seen him do this so close to me on the ground in a few years. I could feel his nervousness and energy through the 4-foot trail reins that connected us. When he was done, I touched his neck and talked to him consolingly, but it was clear that he was still feeling pretty hot and shaken for some reason unbeknownst to me. Was it me? Was I nervous about taking this ride with Wave? I didn't think so, but it was clear we had to work it out before doing anything else.

It took another fifteen minutes of groundwork before I felt ready to safely mount him, but I still wasn't sure what had just happened – was it a bee in his bonnet or something else? There was an afternoon thunderstorm rolling in, as usual, for this time of year, but it looked like we still had a few hours before it would hit us. Was that what had made him so anxious? I couldn't be sure, but I decided to proceed with caution and ride carefully, knowing how he could blow up, seemingly unprovoked.

The trail was easy at first, meandering through some grass and sage fields over rolling hills. It was a small dirt single track, and every now and then we had to pull off the trail to allow a biker or pedestrian to pass. Our map and directions to do "a loop" were a little shady, and when we started seeing splits in the trail, it was hard to know which way to go, so we did the best we could to navigate.

Slowly, the trail changed as it jutted up against the higher country. It got steeper, and the dirt turned to various sheets of rock and scree. Our horses had seen this kind of terrain before, except for Tiki who was carrying our friend, Wave, a nickname he'd had since his youth because he'd learned to ride the waves of the arroyo. She seemed to be doing just fine with an experienced rider on her back in between her two herd mates, who were not phased by this challenging mountain workout.

About 90 minutes into our ride, the slope suddenly fell away to our left as we emerged from a grove of aspen trees revealing a shallow riverbed flowing with fresh snowmelt a thousand feet below. At first the trail had a healthy grip on the mountain, but within a few minutes, it became so narrow and sketchy in places that I knew we would not be able to turn around safely until it was done and that our very lives were dependent on the security of our horses' footing. I'd learned to loosen, or drop, stirrups on such terrain, opting to bail out uphill in the event that they should slip and roll down the mountain.

In high school, I had been riding a trail bareback on my show horse who was never very sturdy on this kind of a trail, and he lost his footing and somersaulted back over me, cartwheeling a few hundred feet beyond where I stopped rolling through the tumbleweed. It was terrifying and humbling. Both of us were shaken up, but aside from a few scratches and cuts, we were unscathed. The memory served to give me a healthy respect for what could happen, especially with a horse that wasn't sure of what it was doing. Tiki's abilities were being tested with little room for error and no experience whatsoever from her first six years of life in the Midwest.

Wave was behind me, and I ventured to ask him how he was doing without looking back. Our heads weigh twelve pounds, and I had learned when jumping horses that even looking down at a jump adds pressure to their shoulder and concentration in getting over the jump – often leading to a refusal, or throwing their balance off to drop a rail. I wanted to do everything I could to support my horse taking the next safe step, and that included keeping my eyes forward and staying in a balanced, neutral position. I'd felt Jet's feet slide out a few times, but we were still holding the trail.

"Remember, the horse doesn't want to fall either," Wave said, sensing my apprehension. I was grateful for this reminder. The same was probably true of my father. Perhaps that was why he had declined our invitations to hit the trail. I respected his decision from this scary height, though I never told him so. It wasn't the first time another father figure had stepped in to share wisdom with me when my dad had been unavailable, and it likely wouldn't be the last. Similarly, I had been sharing my dad with my husband as a substitute father ever since his father took his own life in the first year we were dating, and I'd come to recognize that there is a universal parenting wisdom and identity available to all of us.

At the end of the day, whether or not these parenting figures approved wasn't what mattered most. The most important thing was that I approved of myself and felt I was doing the best I could in the eyes of my partner, immediate family, and God above. They say only six people can sit around the table to immediately influence any decision that you make. The truth was, my parents hadn't had a space at the table of my dreams for many years. I knew they wanted me to live my best life. The question was: if that meant I fell out of step with them, would they still be able to live *their* best lives? When I came to them, they viewed everything as a judge would, and I wondered why? Now that I was also a parent, this paradox plagued me, bringing me face-to-face with these questions once again.

Only time would tell what was really true in all of this, and how that truth would impact the decisions left to be made as we debated the long trek "home" to the flatlands from these high places. After all, you can't stay on the run or on the trail forever. Eventually, we all go home. Sometimes the decision to do so breaks us.

WRITE, RECORD and SHARE

Use the space below to write a few sentences, or pull out your phone and record a short video. Share it with us on social media or through my website!

Whose approval do you seek at the end of the day?

_____

What has seeking their approval kept me from doing?

_____

What has seeking their approval empowered me to do?

_____

Can I decide I approve of myself as I am today?

_____

If I approved of myself wholeheartedly, how would I bring that approval home with me?

_____

Ironically, the people we start out life with, in the homes we were raised in, often stay with us in all that we think and do. But we are our own people with our own unique callings. I would love to hear how you have branched out and honored your roots already, and what you plan to do next!

Mile 4444

July 24th

In the Truck

THE NEWS BROKE ME

"The quieter you become the more you are able to hear."

– Rumi

I was sitting in front of the condo in Telluride, still in the driver's seat, scrolling through Facebook after coming back from getting groceries when the news struck. George's sister had tagged me on a post about a local celebrity death back in the Tetons. The thing was, I knew this woman personally, and she had just taken her own life.

Candy and Cookie, two cousins in a band called The Coors Cousins, were "the heart and soul" of Teton Valley's music scene. They were larger than life celebrities and down-to-earth humans. The two were actually something of a local legend and toured with multiple bands.

Both of them joined my fitness club, and that was how I got to know them better and booked them to play at my own wedding in 2012. Cookie had always struggled with mental health, including mood swings. In the end, only Candy had played at my wedding. Cookie had not, and it was never quite clear exactly what was going on, beyond the fact that she was somehow troubled.

Over the years, Candy maintained her fitness membership and kept me somewhat abreast of the situation. Within our first year of marriage, Cookie had a second child, which explained a lot of the mood swings. This baby died a few months later in its crib when she was out on tour, under her husband's watch. It was horrible, and our whole town was shocked by this.

After that, I saw very little of Cookie, and she withdrew from the limelight. It was just a heartbreaking situation. Ironically, George and I had seen her on one of our last rides in Teton Valley the summer before we moved.

That day, our horses had been skittish about the sound of the dirt bikes whirring closer on the steep hill we were climbing. For a few miles, we had been trying to figure out what the sound was from a distance and had made a few wrong guesses about their origin. The noise was fearsome, and then we saw two dirt bikers switch-backing up the hill at mach speed. We pulled our horses off the trail, shouting to each other about whether or not we should dismount. As the bikes got closer, our horses settled, letting one pass us by. The second bike stopped just past us and removed her helmet, revealing a head of beautiful, long, red hair. It was Cookie! We exchanged small talk, and I think she even petted our horses. Since I hadn't seen her in years, I politely expressed my condolences regarding the passing of her child. Regardless, the focus was on the weather, the sport, and the incredible place we called home.

That was the last time I would ever see her.

Now I was reading about how she'd drowned herself in a lake near Yellowstone. The tears burst forth as I wailed out loud, bawling like a baby. She'd left behind a six-year-old daughter. *A six-year-old daughter.*

It was no secret – with myself, my husband, our therapist, or our children – that I was struggling with post-partum depression. I knew that this trip was a means to journey out of it and make peace with the past, the present, and the future. Here I was facing the fear of not getting better, and the stakes were high for a mother to heal right here and right now.

What had happened? Why couldn't she pull through? For her daughter, if not for herself?

This was not the first time that I was torn apart by suicide. George's father had taken his own life seven years earlier, and I had learned that, like alcoholism, mental illness is a disease. Sometimes "treatment" doesn't work. Many are never able to make their way out of the darkness, ending up locked up, or dead, despite access to rehabs, psychologists and doctors.

Harder still are the pieces of the puzzle left for the remaining friends and relatives to try to put together for the rest of their lives. "What could we have done differently? How could we have seen the signs? What can we do to make sure this never ever happens to anyone we know again?" And that's the thing, there isn't anything that can be done to change it – what's done is done, and the same is true going forward: those who wish to take their lives as a "way out" may find a way to do so. We all have free will.

The horrifying reality was easier to accept when we believed that they were ill, deeply sick, and not in their right minds when they did it, despite their efforts to get better for their loved ones or themselves. At the end of the day, it wasn't personal to anybody else; it was personal to them and their pain, just like this trip was personal to me.

After crying my eyes out in the truck for another 15 or 20 minutes, I pulled out some baby wipes to wipe my tear-stained cheeks and said a prayer for Candy, Cookie's child, Cookie's husband, and all those deeply grieving the loss of this beautiful soul. I prayed that her story would be the incentive those on the edge needed to pull back, and thereby save a life, so that her passing would not be in vain. If there was a streak of depression running through my veins, which I knew there was, I prayed that this could spawn a ray of hope and healing through it.

Then I took a deep breath and went inside to do what needed to be done to prepare dinner for the children and our guests. Living our best life was an antidote, but we would still have to face facts, feelings, and milestones as they came along. I wondered if we should head back north for the celebration of life the following week and change our itinerary home. Realistically, I knew only time would heal this hole in my heart, and that Ruthie or George could not support extending the trip. We would have to heal together and stay the course. The next day, we needed to head back to Snowmass for George to catch his flight the day after.

WRITE, RECORD and SHARE

Use the space below to write a few sentences, or pull out your phone and record a short video. Share it with us on social media or through my website!

Where do you let your deepest feelings out?

_____

How do you cope with loss or sadness?

_____

When did you last cry and why?

_____

Do you place your feelings upon the actions of others?

_____

What do you think happens when you die?

_____

Describe your experience with suicide:

_____

This is a heavy chapter, and sometimes life can feel heavy. What is important is that we find a safe place and safe people to work through it with. If you have not found that person yet, please reach out. If you are experiencing thoughts of suicide, the helpline is 988.

Mile 4699

July 28th

Woody Creek, CO

THE DREAM SITE

"The things that we understand, create silence. The things that we do not, create emotion."

- Kapil Gupta

On the way back from Telluride, we stopped at a trailhead on the top of a mountain pass that we'd scouted on the way over. There were horse campers there, and one of them was driving another "dream trailer." This one was even bigger than the one in the Dakotas, and we couldn't help but introduce ourselves and take a look around.

The owners were an odd couple with at least a short lifetime age difference. It was clear that the man wore the pants and the woman had led horses into their world, but the trailer was a shared vision. He worked as a lawyer, and she focused on "keeping house" and caring for their rescue horses who had portable pens. They'd been camping at this site for the maximum allotted 14 days, maybe longer, and it was clear that they were quite settled in their ways. The trailer was unhooked on stilts to keep it level, and they had all kinds of hookups and generators to be completely self-sufficient up in the high country for a month or more, they explained, having learned what was needed to do that. While George and the man went over additional sewage and gas storage tanks, I got a tour of the interior.

In many ways, this trailer was nicer than the other one, but it was hard to get past the energy of the owners. While the man went back and forth to meet with his relatives 45 minutes away in

Telluride with the truck, the woman clearly never left the site, except on horseback, and her struggles with the disease of alcoholism showed throughout the trailer, which wasn't very clean and was littered with bottles, trash, and dust. So often, we judge people with a clean house as having it all together, and a mess being mentally unstable, but there is always more to the story. Here I was judging silently, so I turned to a silent prayer, placing my hand on my heart, and remembering that "there by the Grace of God go I" and thanked them for the generous tour.

As we rode up the hillside through another exquisite grove of aspen trees, I kept thinking about how everyone finds their way, and I prayed for her recovery. One thing was for sure, as far as horse camping with a viable partner who could afford to get her where she wanted to go, she had clearly arrived. It was between her and God and her partner whether or not the rest would ever come together.

When we got back, the truck was gone. The horses stood in their pens swishing at flies and rubbing their noses on their legs in the heat, and the generator purred. I wondered if she was inside drinking and how many days she had let slide like this. I recognized, humbly, that had things gone differently for me, I very well could be right there beside her, wasting all this sunshine deep in my disease.

Meanwhile, I dared George to take his horse over a creek on the way back, and she collected herself and took a sprawling leap, almost dismounting him. I roared with laughter, and we took a video as he did it again for Ruthie and the girls who were strolling nearby.

At our trailersite, we found a grove to let the horses graze and cool off after our ride while we had a picnic. Grace wanted to sit on Tiki while she ate her sandwich. I sat with my back against a perfectly positioned aspen tree and nursed Dani. From this vantage point, I could see that the rear tires on the trailer looked like they might be out of alignment again. All the adults took a look, and after we loaded them up, we took turns checking it out for the first few minutes of turns out of the campsite.

It wasn't anything like before, but we agreed we probably needed to get it checked out before making the long haul back home. I knew there were trailer dealers in the area, and I spent that night researching alternative options. Perhaps our trailer had run its course. It was almost paid off, but we had long since outgrown it, and this trip might have been more than it could handle.

The trailer had been custom-built for a family in Tennessee and sold "used" on the builder's website. I'd found it searching for "built out" trailers with sleeping quarters for people and diagonal stalls, which are supposed to be better for horses hauling long distances. It had other features I didn't know to think about, which all these dream trailers also had, like a separate tack closet so your living quarters don't smell like dusty, sweaty horse tack. For many years, George and I had lived out our camping dreams all over the Tetons, but it just wasn't big enough for our future needs, or even those of the present. I'd worked hard to make it work, but two breakdowns and many suspicions later, this dream was starting to feel like a nightmare.

Something needed to change. The question was whether it needed to change now or later. Furthermore, we were headed back to Pitkin county, and I knew we couldn't keep our horses at The Soft Spot again. A friend of mine had volunteered to let us use the pasture where she was a caretaker, but I hadn't been comfortable taking her up on it. Similar to the situation with making that call again for the Telluride horse Park, I was ready now.

She asked her boss, he said yes, and the next thing we knew, we were headed into a new stretch of territory that I'd never been to before, with much greener pastures. The horses would have their own hill to graze with fresh water and my friend living in a cabin adjoining them. Our family's house was further than the last place we stayed, but felt closer because we had friends on site with the animals, and they were totally at home in a greener pasture.

George flew out the next afternoon, which was a Sunday, after we returned from Telluride. I was sorry to see him go. I missed him already. It was a heavy load to get all of this home by myself, which felt more like a nightmare than the dream I envisioned, but it was the only way we had figured out how to make it happen. I was alone in having to make the decisions about the trailer and, possibly, buying a new one, if it came to that.

Ruthie was starting to get anxious to get home to see her husband and her family in time for her birthday. This was the longest they had ever been apart, and it was understandable. We also agreed that safety needed to come first, so I woke up Monday morning and called a few RV and trailer repair numbers in the phonebook. Most mechanics were either busy or not answering their phones until I got ahold of one in Glenwood Springs, about an hour back up the valley with the trailer in tow. They were willing to squeeze us in on their lunch break, given the circumstances.

Gratefully, Ruthie and I split duties regarding the girls, and I took Dani and the trailer, along with covering the horses that evening, while Ruthie had some one-on-one time with Grace and took care of laundry. We agreed that the next day would be a rest day for all of us, and possibly a trailer shopping day, or maintenance, if need be. I'd worked a lot of flexibility into all aspects of our itinerary, but I could feel that the trip was getting long and needed to end sooner than later. We could not stay out here in this adventure state forever, and I knew that.

Sure, there was the trailer to deal with, but there was also something else in my soul that was uneasy. Why had I come all this way trying to make peace with my past in order to bring it into the present and create joy for our future? In many ways, I felt more confused than ever. Despite the feelings of empowerment and God's grace that had surrounded us throughout our journey, it still seemed I was alone in this dream with my children and loved ones in tow.

As I drove down the valley, I began to cry, imagining where the road could go, and where it had taken Cookie. I cried for her, for her family, for myself and my family, and all the things we'd left behind. Sometimes the future, even when you know where you are going and who you are going with, still looks scary. It was too big to solve on the way. I needed to go home to face the music, but first I had to make sure my "instrument" was in tune, so I took it to one last mechanic for a final tune up. Spoiler alert: nothing was wrong with it.

WRITE, RECORD and SHARE

Use the space below to write a few sentences, or pull out your phone and record a short video. Share it with us on social media or through my website!

Have you ever wasted time by worrying?

_____

How do you work through deep feelings of sadness?

_____

When you feel truly alone, are you at home in that feeling?

_____

What would it look like to be at home regardless of what happened?

_____

To stay confident when I feel insecure about how my home will work out, I try saying this to myself:

_____

If you have read this far, you are recognizing that you are building your own spiritual toolkit to feel at home wherever you go and whatever you do, come what may. This is one of the greatest gifts of this book — helping you come home to your own wisdom. Often, the greatest gifts come when we hit the bottom. Please reach out and share it with the rest of us!

Mile 4832

August 1st

Boulder, CO

THE CURSE OF NIWOT

"They have me singing in a reformatory. My singing would be enough to get me in, but I'd never be able to sing my way out."

– David Stenn

As the sun rose on one of our last days in the mountains, I was grateful for Ruthie and the rhythm we had going now. We'd been through enough storms to know how to weather what was left, or so we thought. The trailer had checked out after all, and we were good to go, but still had the journey of 1000 miles ahead of us. The next four nights in four different states would test us, from CO, to NE, to IA, to IL.

The most technical terrain would come first as we made our way through the rocky mountains down to the foothills. I had tried to plan our stops so that I would be driving the scarier stretches of I-70, but the next thing we knew, we had passed all possible exits and Ruthie was behind the wheel as we climbed Vail pass. Both of us were saying prayers and scouting pullover options, but nothing looked good or safe given the high-speed traffic and steep pitches. Unless it was an emergency, pulling over to switch drivers was more likely to cause an emergency situation on these slopes.

Of course, Ruthie was also warmed up now and had been driving this trailer for weeks on simpler terrain routes. It appeared she was ready for the challenge. I coached her from the rear passenger seat between my children. "Take your foot off the gas and let her coast down this hill... Feather the brakes if gravity takes you over 65 here.... Nice work!"

When we finally reached the top of Vail Pass and pulled over at the rest stop, both of us exhaled in unison. It was a sigh of relief and triumph. Ruthie had now qualified for "Advanced Placement."

I'd never stopped at this rest stop – perhaps because I was always in a hurry, or maybe it hadn't yet been built when I last lived in Colorado. The place was beautiful. It had picnic benches and trails to walk your dog, along with a great lineup of bathrooms and vending machines.

While Grace walked Chadeaux, I took pictures and soaked up the scenery. The population of Colorado has the lowest BMI in the nation, and being in a place like this reminded me why. Even the rest stops were designed for self-care and exercise. Everyone liked to get out, for "The hills are alive with the sound of music."

As we snacked, I became saddened, once again, that this was coming to a close. I had to keep my eye on the ball and "keep moving forward," as my grandfather was famous for saying to my aunt after she made a failed investment decision. Life, like this trip, is long, and does not last forever. My responsibility was to continue to safely see it through to the end, moving in a "Godly" way. In recovery rooms, they have an acronym for God: "good orderly direction." Even in my sadness, I could hold a compass to that bearing.

Having a good friend or two to meet down the road helped. Back in the day, I had more friends than I could count in Boulder, but most of us had scattered since college. A few had returned or moved there from other places where I had known them.

We would be staying with Bonita. She and I had been caretakers back in Wilson, Wyoming on the same property where I had taken care of Jet. Now she lived on another caretaker property with a few chickens of her own. Grace was crazy about chickens.

Although I'd spent a lot of time in Boulder, she lived in a part I had never been to before, and I was excited to find a new spot. The one-acre grass pasture wasn't exactly made for horses. In fact, the fence line was a mish-mash of 3 different kinds of fencing, including a white picket one from the adjoining neighbors and a wire mesh fence along the front. I walked the fence line and decided that it would be okay for a night, though the horses would likely test it if we stayed longer than that. They would have grass and space to run and stretch their legs, which is what we needed.

While Bonita filled up a water tub for us, I went to unload the horses. I could tell that they were unseasonably hot, and when I opened the trailer, I saw why: one of the two hay bales I had stuffed into the back of the trailer had burst open. Poor Solita was drowning in hay up to her belly and all throughout her stomach, which created a convection, like a down blanket or fire under her belly. She had sweat painted across the length of her body.

Similar to hypothermia, the best treatment for heat stroke is to remove them from the elements immediately, if possible, and reverse the overheating by cooling back to a more moderate temperature. Ruthie took her over to Bonita to get hosed off with water, then scraped dry to cool her. Leaving the wet water on there would also serve to make her hotter – there was an art to all of this that we had learned with similar mistakes.

Jet was next, and though he was also hot, he wasn't as bad as Solita who had had all the fuel underneath her body at the back where the hay bale had probably turned over under her foot on those mountain passes sometime in the past 5 hours. We hosed him off anyway for good measure. Lastly, we unloaded Tiki, and she appeared to be fine, with hardly a drop of sweat on her golden coat, so we proceeded to give her only a light spray for fun.

Then we let all three horses go in the pasture at once, after walking them around so they could see the perimeter of this strange pasture and we could be sure they'd seen it under our lead before running through it in their excitement. They were thrilled to be out of the trailer and set to work running the whole area over once more before settling down to graze.

Happy with that, I went back to clean the trailer out, offering the manure to Bonita for fertilizer. While she and Ruthie worked on that with her wheelbarrow, I proceeded to stuff the hay bags for the following day with all of the offending hay, but there was just too much. Luckily, we had a tarp and were able to save some of it, waiting to wrap it the next day in such a way that it would not be a fire hazard – hay can be tricky that way.

All of us needed showers, but Bonita and I were going to hit a meeting together and grab pizzas while Ruthie took care of herself and the girls. I could shower later. But first, we had to spend some time playing with the chickens. Grace memorized the names of every one and said them in her cute toddler voice. After setting a few ground rules about playing with them while we were gone, we set off.

The meeting was filled with people I did not know but felt familiar with, having a common purpose and sharing a belief, or hope anyway, in a shared solution. Then, suddenly, I recognized the voice of a woman sharing. She had changed the trajectory of my relationship with my body in early adulthood and continued to be one of my greatest life long teachers.

Her name was Ramona, but everyone called her "Rambo" because she was a fit and fierce personal trainer. In college, I had signed up for a 10-pack package to get fit. At that point, I already knew that the idea of being discontent with my body, body shaming, or focusing on diet and weight loss were not for me. But I'd unintentionally succeeded in losing a bunch of weight after I broke my neck, and it had started to pack back on six months later as I got into new routines my freshman year. I wanted to learn how to get strong, and if that also meant I could stay a size 8-10, that would be great, but strength was my focus.

Rambo taught me how to fall in love with exercise. From the endorphins to the community of people caring for their bodies and chasing that adrenaline high, I had found my tribe. She literally changed my life by teaching me how to adopt these habits and seek out ways so that I enjoyed exercising for life; regardless of circumstances, peaks, or valleys, a gym could be found anywhere and was actually inside the mind, I later realized.

After the meeting, I nearly cried as I conveyed all of this to her. I even told her I had called the gym years later trying to find her, and they said no one by that name worked there. She laughed, because she now owned the gym and asked who had answered the phone! We both chuckled and posed for Righteous

Babe photos, then went on our way.

It felt like a full circle, like Niwot had promised. According to legend, he was the Native American Chief who said that anyone who came to Boulder and felt her beauty would be cursed in that, no matter where they moved in life, they would forever circle back to the Flatirons, captured by her spell. This had proved true, for here we were, spellbound by old friends and new adventures.

Somehow, I knew this was the beginning of the closure I needed. When we got back with the pizzas, Ruthie had already unhooked the truck and was ready to go — she had a friend she wanted to see and stay with for the night in Boulder. I wondered if she would come back on time, and if she didn't, whether or not I would care. After all, I was right where I wanted to be.

In the morning, I woke up to the sound of a rooster crowing. Both girls were sleeping with me in the trailer, and I took a few selfies of us all together. George was missing, but somehow it felt so right to be together, just us girls, right now.

As they snoozed on, I wondered what time Ruthie would show up. Then I wondered, again, if I cared. I felt like we had all the time in the world, and I wanted to soak up this last morning in Colorado with my friend, eating her fresh chicken eggs and pulling horse spirit cards.

Just then I heard a growling of the diesel engine parking on the street outside. Ruthie was early!

Through the screen door, we greeted each other, as I had to move things around before being able to open the door and was still in my pajamas.

"You didn't want to have breakfast with your friend?" I asked.

"Nope – we were all done. I wanted to give my energy to the trip today!"

Somehow, this enthusiasm made me feel more excited about getting going as well. Her loyalty confirmed what was to come and breathed new life into my waning resolve, bringing us full circle in our next round out of Boulder. It was time to leave the mountains and head home.

WRITE, RECORD and SHARE

Use the space below to write a few sentences, or pull out your phone and record a short video. Share it with us on social media or through my website!

What thoughts do you think again and again?

_____

Who are the top three teachers in your life who have helped you come home to your own wisdom?

_____

How has exercise brought you home in your body?

_____

When it is time to go home, who keeps me going to get there?

_____

If you have not already actively started exercising as a practice towards whatever dream you have chosen to tackle next, now is the time to get started! I'm a lifelong health expert and have many programs to offer in this department. Exercise is one of my favorite ways to come home to myself — please join me!

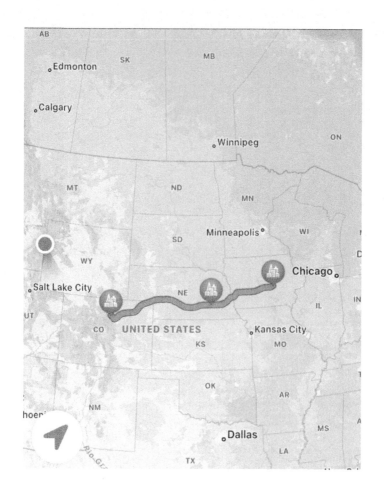

Mile 4832- 5719

August 2-4

Colorado to Iowa

GOD ON SPEED DIAL

"If you face God in prayer and silence, God will speak to you. Then you will know that you are nothing. It is only when you realize your nothingness, your emptiness, that God can fill you with Himself. Souls of prayer are souls of great silence."

— Mother Teresa

Heading east from Boulder along I-70, our next two stops would be repeat stays from when we had first moved from the Tetons to the Chicago area five years before. I wondered if they would remember us. I'd learned to find all these people using "Horsemotel.com" and quickly accessed a range of characters and comrades.

The Nebraska stop was one of my favorites – in the middle of the country at a convenient location about 10 minutes off the interstate was a huge working farm. The man was a pilot and a veterinarian who often flew to his clients because they were all so remote, so they had a runway on the land as well. The wife mostly raised the children, cared for the animals, and ran the Airbnb apartment that we would rent again.

Just as before, the room was clean and quiet, attached to the barn with its own bathroom, a coffee maker, and two stags on the wall. One of them had been tagged in the same year that I was born. I hadn't noticed that before, but this time, we had a long stare at one another, me recognizing that he had been dead and mounted on a wall for the same amount of time that I had been alive and traveling the earth. It seemed a strange solace in the midst of this pilgrimage home.

Now I got to see this place with new eyes as Ruthie and the girls explored and introduced themselves to every chicken, goat, horse, and critter available. The hosts barely remembered us, but were friendly enough and happy that we were repeat customers. In the morning, we also discovered two new foals, and Grace had her first run in with an electric fence which was, of course, shocking – a lesson most of us never need to repeat.

As she cried, I held her close and stroked her hair, talking about what had happened and that it never needed to happen again as long as we gave those fences space, just like the animals do. Eventually, she calmed down and regained interest in some Goldfish and said goodbye to the chicks with Ruthie while I loaded up the horses.

We went to a diner five minutes down the road and sat in a booth. While we waited for our pancakes, I drove the horses to the trucker gas station and filled up the truck. It was fun to be the littlest guy in the row for a change as I watched the 18- and 26-wheelers pull in and out beside me. Everyone smiled, not used to seeing a woman seemingly by herself filling up with her horses – if only they knew that there was another woman and small children with us, too!

Back on the road, Grace noticed that the scenery had changed, and she asked why we didn't live in the mountains again. I wished I had a good answer. All I knew was that we were moving in the right direction, and that we had to learn to be at home wherever we were, with each other, and with God, who is everywhere.

She seemed satisfied, and somehow, I knew that it was only

going to get better in some ways and worse in others as we got closer to Chicago. Our next stop was only about five hours away, near Des Moines, and it was another one of my favorites. It was a small operation, similar to ours, tucked into a residential area with just a few horses left on the property and plenty of extra private pasture to rent out to those passing through as a result.

We had to stop and pull the horses out for a picnic on the way there, because the drive ended up being longer than we remembered, but it was worth the haul, because the hosts were just as dear as I remembered them being, and they also remembered us, which was touching. The old man had a grandchild living with him now, and I vaguely recalled a story about a daughter who struggled with drug addiction being in the picture. I wondered if she was still in it or not, given the circumstances. He had clearly grown into the grandpa role, and evidence of his enthusiasm could be found all over the property, from miniature tractors, to pink bicycles, lawn toys, and kiddie pools. Our girls were in heaven. But best of all, he had a miniature horse who had just had a foal. It was the size of a large puppy and so cute and cuddly.

There was no space for us to stay on property this time, so we would go to a hotel nearby after we got the horses settled in the bright green pasture. Considering safety first, as we were switching feed, I assessed our history. Prevention is always the best medicine. Essentially, we had "worked" them with 5-6 hours on the road, one of the best antidotes to colic for a horse, and a common solution among vets is a trailer ride. They'd get one more tomorrow, so we decided we were good to go.

On our host's porch, I could see a sign that said: "Prayer, the original wireless connection." Or something like that. I connected with "source" and knew we were on the right path, going home, now, to reunite with our loved ones. Then we went to the same Mexican restaurant I had with George when we first moved East with the horses in 2015. The girls ate a whole bowl of guacamole together before melting down completely. Ruthie and I ended up taking our meals to go.

WRITE, RECORD and SHARE

Use the space below to write a few sentences, or pull out your phone and record a short video. Share it with us on social media or through my website!

How do you know when it's time to just go home?

When do your parenting instincts kick in?

What was your home life like growing up?

How did your parents arrange accommodations for you and your animals growing up?

Is your home where you want it to be?

Our homes are so closely linked to our upbringing, and sometimes a complete 180 from how we were raised. This work is a beautiful opportunity to embrace all that you have been, all that you are, and all that you are becoming.

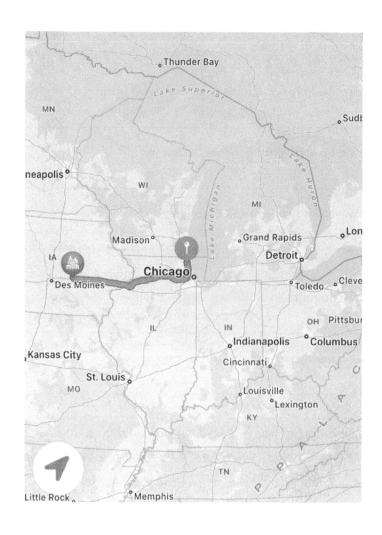

Mile 6000

August 5th

Back to Hidden Ranch

THERE'S NO PLACE LIKE HOME

"Home is where the heart is."

-J.T. Bickford

What happened when we came home?

Well, similar to when we left the midwest, we returned to the boiling summer temperatures of literal "hell" for our horses. Traveling in a hot metal box on blacktop with high humidity is not for sissies, and we returned with more experience, and the same grit and determination we started with to keep everyone safe. This meant pulling over to get the horses out to cool the trailer down and offer them water twice before entering the Chicago area. But first, we started late.

Toddlers sleeping in new hotel environments with all their favorite people in the same room turned out not to be at all conducive to a good night's sleep, and made for a delayed start from Des Moines. We missed the 3 am alarm going off, and it was close to 5 am when I woke up, meaning we were all going to be 2 hours deeper into the heat of the day. Anticipating another battle with horses and heat, we moved through those early morning hours in a haze, getting coffee and sandwiches from Starbucks right as they opened. Something was wrong with the order, but it wasn't important enough to go back and fix, so we took what we got.

Ruthie's curling iron and makeup were laid out in the hotel

bathroom to enhance her beauty for her husband, and their first six-week reunion. I laughed, recognizing that my reality was so far away from hers in terms of things I'd be waking up early to do on a day we were hauling horses across the country in high heat. All I could think about was coffee and going through the motions to make sure all the animals and humans were safe with the heat. I'm pretty sure I splashed water on my face and put on deodorant, but that was about it.

Still, I admired her resolve and focus on being more than presentable to her husband. Since we missed the time in the hotel in front of a mirror, she beautified herself in the backseat with Grace "ooh-ing" and "aah-ing," and asking questions about what she was doing. It was pretty cute to witness this lesson – this lesson on beauty between a girl and a young woman.

Sometimes I give beauty and makeup a bad name. The truth is, I love a good lipstick and smooth face as much as the next man or woman. However, I have other things, like horses and adventure, and above all, being present and relatable to others, that I hold in even higher esteem. This is the paradox of fashion and aesthetics. I love a clean house, but agree that "a clean house may be the sign of a life wasted." In reality, this is one of the basics that we must attend to for our health. We also all have different baselines for what is needed, what is acceptable, and what makes us most comfortable in our homes and on our faces.

There is a shift that happens when we become comfortable either way, when we allow ourselves to love and be loved and seen with or without makeup. I come from a mountain culture where most women don't have time, space, or energy for this kind of ritual, and they are the most beautiful, authentic, gritty, wrinkled, and sensuous women I know! Seeing these gorgeous mountain mamas show up and age gracefully has given me a vision for how I am, how I want to be, and how I carry the message to my children. I am at home in my body as it is.

Like the mountains and the horses, we are real. We have a history of seasons and experiences, landslides and caretakers upon our bodies. Some mountains get carved away, repaved, and moved to make new hills or gentler slopes, like the cosmetic surgery that took place on Moran Faces at Jackson Hole Resort a few years ago. The Native Americans said that moving the earth disturbed the spirits, and pointed to this as being the reason certain things went wrong there. If I hadn't blown my knee on that spot, I might not have paid this kind of theory any mind, but I did, and it opened up my range of possibilities around what might be true when humans move mountains for their own economic reasons.

When women focus too deeply on their beauty, a similar beast is raised up in the ego. For men, it's often their careers that they focus on. Suddenly, they turn around, and their wife and children are all grown up, or gone, and they hardly know them, despite all the success that was wrought from the late nights and long hours. Similarly, when women become obsessed with their appearance, competing with other women who appear thinner, or younger, or more desirable for any reason, they lose out on the heart of the matter. This becomes a self-fulfilling prophecy towards unhappiness when we go so far down the rabbit hole of beauty or money that we lose sight of the simple things that make something beautiful or expensive: craftsmanship of the master craftsman, whom I choose to call God, or the gifts God has given a human to create something with their lives and money, which are the most beautiful and priceless things of all. We can get so focused on the external home that we live in that we forget to attend to our inner home and miss out on the return to a sense of homeostasis in the body and talents God gave us.

The moment we embrace our bodies as our forever home until death do us part, that is the moment that we begin to truly love and take responsibility for our thoughts about our bodies, especially as it naturally waxes and wanes, grows and fades. We have a part to play in terms of how we show up to one another. For example, "with or without deodorant" makes a big difference when sweating in society! However, a little lipstick on or off doesn't break any deals for me, personally. Maybe that's a city thing?

As we hauled toward the city, I could feel that magnetic pull in my heart to be with my partner and began communicating with him. We were also starving and needed lunch. Classically, there was no food in the house, so he went to pick up Panera for us, and we headed straight home to get the horses out of the trailer and into their safe pasture. This exchange helped me recognize that while we were all out on this "trip of a lifetime" with all the highs and lows therein, for much of the time, he was entertaining customers and working hard.

As I entered the concrete jungle, I felt that empty pit in my stomach. On a gut level, I missed seeing the grass and the mountains and the natural landscape that speak to my soul. I worked so hard to get away from all of this, I thought – why on earth am I here?!?! But I also felt that familiar pull towards a home of our own, and the dream of unconditional family love. I looked past the pavement, and the traffic, and the last preserves of nature hanging tightly to their curbs in suburbia, and I saw us, traveling through space, nearing the end of a very long journey.

As we drove down our quarter-mile driveway, I felt the transition from the city through the portal back to the sanctity of the five acre parcel we called home.

Seeing our horses get out of the trailer and step back onto their own property was a beautiful thing to witness. They blinked, then rolled, and looked around, taking in all that was familiar and different, because they were somehow made new, embodying the truth that we can never step into the same river twice. Looking at each other, there was a mutual understanding of freedom as the horses embraced all that we had worked so hard to build for them, and they released us from the stress of trying to find it along the way. I knew that they saw me, and my family, and Ruthie reuniting with her husband at our deepest truth. Could they see the little girl in my heart hoping to stay out west? Or not? Could they see my hope that, after all of this, I was also finally home, too, in myself, and able to let go of what was in the rearview?

Only time would tell. This day was our "happily ever after." Someday, "over the rainbow," another adventure would be born. Our conception of home would continue to shift and change, ultimately reminding us that home is not a house, or a zip code, but a way of being inside of ourselves, and with others, wherever we are. Finally, we could just stay home - it was time, and we were ready .

WRITE, RECORD and SHARE

Use the space below to write a few sentences, or pull out your phone and record a short video. Share it with us on social media or through my website!

What do you need to be ready to just stay home?

_____

Just one question to leave you with in the last chapter – and it sums it up. The real secret we all learned in the pandemic is to be at peace at home and on the journey. Through the writing and reflection of both, we have embraced the paradoxical nature of all that we are, all that we were, and all that we are becoming. Now we begin a new story…

Epilogue

"The development of loving kindness is a demanding practice that requires time. However, see if you can cultivate some part of loving kindness toward yourself, other people in your life, and the natural world around you every day... loving kindness for all life on the earth is the ultimate result of the deepest understanding of the unity of life."

– Claire Thompson

"So, why did you do it?" my friend asked me after reading this book early on.

"Honestly, I still don't even know," I said.

"Was it all just to escape?" she asked.

I paused for half a second before answering. "Yes, actually – I think that is exactly what it was." My friend had suddenly connected the dots for me. But escape from what? Essentially, I was escaping all of my responsibilities back at the ranch and the dread of staying home.

Yet, I believe "the masters master the basics." If this is true, then the real goal is mastering all we have at home, *and* our desire to escape it all for something else, like the trip of a lifetime. This is why the adventure paradox exists – because we cannot be in that "big state" of adventure all the time. Even when we are on a Grand Canyon 21-day rafting expedition, the truth is that the class 10 rapids are only a few minutes of every day. The adrenaline of adventure is a natural part of us, and we crave those few minutes as an escape from whatever else we were thinking or feeling.

This is why great art exists, so that we might really feel something just by looking at it or experiencing it through a medium, like film or sculpture. Now that I have finally written the book and worked through all of the things that happened, and how I felt about them, I recognized that this journey was one very long meditation on fear. I feared, at the deepest level, that I would wake up one day and my children would be fully grown, and we'd still be living in the greater Chicago metropolitan area, and they never would have had the perspective of being a mountain person in their youth. So here we are, five years later, and I am still feeling that way, and the question is: why haven't we moved yet?

Great question! Moving has been described as synonymous with the stress of losing a loved one. We were almost two years out from the journey you just read about when we entered the pandemic. At first, I considered taking another adventure, but I recognized how stretched our family was, not to mention the nation, in trying to make sense of what was happening. Whatever it was felt really big to all of us. Instead, I settled into staying home and writing this book. Always looking for and actively seeking the next thing meant that I had a lot of unfinished internal goals, and writing the book was one of them. I wasn't the only one. My editor shared with me that her business was bombarded by "COVID books" written by other creatives who were finally home long enough to get the thing they said they would do done. Moreover, you can see why I could hardly even talk about what had happened for the following year – it was just so intense, and I was still processing what it all meant. I also had a lot of fear about writing about my friends and family who shaped many of the thoughts, experiences, and stories that transpired: how do you do that?

Now, I know. It just came to me. I know why I had to do it, and why I had to wait so long before writing the book and getting the mission to bring others into partnership with horses and themselves through adventures. It was through writing and editing the book that I found my own answers.

This book is not about me. It is about all of us. Every one of us has an essential nature. If we are aligned, at our essence, then things seem to work out. When we are not, then everything we do seems "off," and life feels like a struggle. It does not have to be this way. There is always another way. Your dreams matter, and the things holding you back can be released. You are not a tree. You can move if you want to!

I've let go of the need to prove myself and my worth wherever I am – especially in the writing of this book. It's a bad habit that can still creep in, but I have learned to catch myself now when it happens and change course. I'm also clearer about letting go of the outcome – the thought that I could go all the way to the mountains and return as the lone ranger to tell everyone all about it was naive. When I let go and just became the person I believed I would be if we were out West, incredible things happened. I dressed, talked, and felt more like myself. People wanted to get to know me and get to know more about the horses. I began teaching again. My children continued to grow up, and they brought their friends with them to learn together at the ranch. We built many more beautiful memories and managed to spend almost two months out West every year beginning in 2021. But, like the adrenaline of the horse road trip, it was not sustainable, and we knew that, although we were getting closer to what we really wanted with this hybrid version, there was still another way and another dream to be realized.

First, we bought a bigger horse trailer – one that would fit our entire family and make it possible to run workshops on the road and horse camp again. By doing this, I accessed a higher level of ownership towards our wealth, using it for good, instead of letting it use me. Then we saw an opportunity to put our house on the market and went through the physical, emotional, and spiritual work of letting go of all that we had created to prepare it for someone else to make memories in. As another itinerary out west unfolded, we saw that we could make the decision to make it a one-way adventure where we weren't just moving in the right direction, but we were simply moving. This all happened in the last few months as I have been editing this book and designing the signature workshop to go with it.

They say that when you write your memoir, you relive every chapter of your life, and this has been true for me. As I went through each story, I could feel that the longing to be grounded in the mountains was the thing holding me back, still to this day. I was the one making excuses for why we needed to be here and not there. I was the one with the power to change the narrative, too, and so I did. Actually, we did, together, gently and methodically, considering the highest good for all of our animals and our children. We focused on who we are and what is best for us. Then, George and I began harmoniously writing our next chapter.

In the age of the "infodemic," it is easy to let comparison, judgment, shame, and critique alter our basic need to be okay as we are. What matters is not how much money, or power, or access we have. Those are all simply "stories." What matters is what we know, in our souls, about who we are at our core, without trying to hide anything from anyone, and what we do with that knowledge. Through this practice, we engage in an essential kindness, the kind of kindness that makes the world go round, and that kindness is also known as love. Often, we have blocked ourselves from giving and receiving love, and I have learned that forgiveness is the key to love. When I forgave myself for what I really wanted, I could move on. If I could do it, you can, too.

We may love our children, our bodies, our families, our friends, our geography, our homes, our jobs, our animals, "our God," or our places of worship; but the most essential thing is not just to love ourselves in relation to all things, but to be kind to ourselves. It is when we create a separation from ourselves with anything that we not only become unkind to each other, or to it, but we lose the opportunity to be kind to ourselves. When we allow for our gifts to shine ever more brightly, and move away from things that diminish them, then we learn to serve at our highest vibration. This is often the dance of forgiveness, and it doesn't make someone better or worse, but it allows for love and kindness, and what puts you in the best place to be kind to yourself and others.

By tapping into this kindness, I have discovered the strength to take massive action in order to not only be kind to myself but to be kind to others, too. I have dreamed big dreams, prayed big prayers, and received big answers. Currently, I am in the process of preparing for a three-month odyssey all across the USA promoting this book and running workshops out of the dream horse trailer. I've recognized the vulnerability, the expansiveness, the possibility, and purpose that comes from getting to connect to someone who is literally living their dreams is good for everyone – if I can do it, you can do it, too. The kindest thing we can do is help others to do the same, to the best of our abilities, taking whatever gifts and blessings we were born with with us, humbly and wisely. If you are struggling with the next step, that is a good start. Just take one – it could be an inch in the direction of your dreams, then another. What is holding us back is all in our minds – our perception of reality, not in what actually is.

The truth is, it begins at home, because "home" is where our essential nature is born and raised. What we take with us when we leave is our "haul," and what we choose to do with it is where we "go big." If there is one point I hope I have been able to drive home in this book, it is that the change starts with you being gentle with yourself and others on the adventure of life.

"Hindsight is 20/20," as they say, and when I sat down and finally polished this story off to share with others, I was able to see it. I could see that when we cast our dreams for a brighter tomorrow, and buy the big rig, or get the puppy, or leave the job to pursue our own ambitions, we take a known risk. Feelings will be felt, and some of them do hurt. This is the great paradox of life, that to feel the highest highs, we must also feel the lowest lows. When we risk it all, we sometimes fail... but sometimes we fly. We all made promises to ourselves to change the trajectory of our lives when the pandemic started, to "do something" and "be somebody." If you are reading this, it is not too late. Get back on the horse. Take the trip. Write the book. God will meet you there!

WRITE, RECORD and SHARE

Use the space below to write a few sentences, or pull out your phone and record a short video. Share it with us on social media or through my website!

Now, the paradoxical question is:

Have you done the work to be ready yet?

If you have not, I invite you to join me on the journey – together, we can go the distance.

Acknowledgements:

This book would not have taken place if it weren't for my Chicago playwright friend prodding a group to get after that writing project in the pandemic. That was the prompt, followed by the incredible Nim Stant who showed me how to publish, and even sent me a dream in the writing of this book when I was faltering to "Be The Person You Said You Would Be" (who follows through on the things you say you'll do). I'd like to thank Nim's publishing team, for Net's creativity, Jas's willingness to try new things, and especially my amazing editor, Caroline Barnhill, who spent countless hours helping me make this book what it was meant to be. Special thanks to Rachelt Haft, Aneta Kuzma, Wendy von Oech and Snehal Vadvalkar, and all my early readers – your feedback elevated this story. Rachel, this trip would not have happened without your dedication to the mission – thank you, and I bless you as you begin your own adventures with your children. Finally, I want to thank my adventure partner and husband, George Myers, for everything that you are, all we have done and all we will do – I truly believe the best is yet to come! To my daughters, you helped me see where I needed to shift to be happy, reminding me why that matters with love and kindness. I journey for and with you, my darlings. THANK YOU, GOD, Jesus, the animals, and all my spiritual guides who carried us through it all – I am nothing without you.

"Oh my God, what if you wake up some day, and you're 65, or 75, and you never got your memoir or novel written, or you didn't go swimming in those warm pools and oceans all those years because your thighs were jiggly and you had a nice big comfortable tummy; or you were just so strung out on perfectionism and people-pleasing that you forgot to have a big juicy creative life, of imagination and radical silliness and staring off into space like when you were a kid? It's going to break your heart. Don't let this happen."

— Anne Lamott

About the Author

Cat Caldwell Myers lives on a small horse farm with her family. When they are on the road, they all live out of a dream horse trailer with bunk beds. Cat is the host of The Adventure Paradox Podcast and is available for speaking engagements. She teaches mothers, caretakers, and women to dream bigger through adventures with animals. Find out more at: www.catcaldwellmyers.com

Made in the USA
Monee, IL
21 September 2023

43109106R00144